MORAL FORMATION IN THE PARISH

MORAL FORMATION IN THE PARISH

With Your Whole Heart Turn To God
(Tobit 13:6)

Anthony J. Ciorra, PhD
James Keating, PhD

ALBA·HOUSE alba house NEW·YORK

SOCIETY OF ST. PAUL, 2187 VICTORY BLVD., STATEN ISLAND, NEW YORK 10314

ST PAULS

Library of Congress Cataloging-in-Publication Data

Ciorra, Anthony J. and James Keating.
   Moral formation in the parish: with your whole heart, turn to God
   / Anthony J. Ciorra and James Keating.
      p.   cm.
   Includes bibliographical references.
   ISBN 0-8189-0815-7
   1. Christian ethics — Study and teaching. 2. Christian education.
3. Catholic Church — Education. 4. Catholic Church — Doctrines — Study
and teaching.   I. Keating, James.   II. Title.
   BJ1249.C43   1998
   241'.042'071—dc21   98-5365
                                                           CIP

Produced and designed in the United States of America by the
Fathers and Brothers of the Society of St. Paul,
2187 Victory Boulevard, Staten Island, New York 10314,
as part of their communications apostolate.

ISBN: 0-8189-0815-7

Printing Information:

Current Printing - first digit   1   2   3   4   5   6   7   8   9   10

Year of Current Printing - first year shown

1998   1999   2000   2001   2002   2003   2004   2005

DEDICATION

For my nieces and nephews:

Anthony and Ellen, Joseph and Carolyn,
Kathy and David, Lewis, Marilyn, and Christopher.

A.J.C.

For

Marianne, Kristoffer, and Jonathan.

J.K.

CONTENTS

ACKNOWLEDGMENTS

We would like to acknowledge those who have helped us in the writing of this book. We are grateful to the people who took time to read the drafts and revisions and make comments on them: James Hanigan, PhD, of Duquesne University; Mark Huddy, JD, Director of the Office of Social Concerns, Stephanie Jenemann, Director of the Office of Family Life, and Leslie Young, PhD, Director of the Ministry Formation Office, all in the Diocese of Columbus, Ohio; Judy McElwee, Director of Adult Education at St. Anthony Parish, Columbus; Rev. Frank Lane of Columbus; and Rev. Michael T. Grey, C.S.Sp., PhD, of Duquesne University. Thank you also to Sr. Kathleen Flanagan, Sr. Ellen Joyce, and Dr. Laura Winters, faculty members at the College of St. Elizabeth, Morristown, New Jersey, for offering their invaluable suggestions and advice. The librarians at the Pontifical College Josephinum and the College of St. Elizabeth were always accommodating and competent in providing many of the resources needed for this work. A special thanks must go to the work of Elizabeth Kampmeier, MDiv, Theology Faculty Research Assistant at the Josephinum. Her work is exemplary and professional; she is theologically astute and a pleasure to have as a colleague. Special thanks also to Diane Leffler and the staff of the Center for Theological and Spiritual Development at the College of St. Elizabeth for their support and encouragement in helping with the details of preparing this work, and to the Sisters of Mercy in Philadelphia for their technical assistance in preparing the manuscript.

* * * * *

We are grateful to the publishers of *Emmanuel* for giving us permission to reprint portions of a previously published essay: James Keating, PhD, "Pastoral Moral Renewal," *Emmanuel* 102 (September 1996): 424-433, 438-9.

PREFACE

The Catholic parish is entering a critical time regarding the moral formation of its members. Many pastoral leaders who heralded "a new morality" are nearing retirement as their thirty-odd years of ministry come to a close.[1] It is time to make decisions about how a new generation of pastoral ministers will approach their role in the moral development of parishioners. Will we educate people in the moral truths of Catholicism in order to facilitate a personal appropriation of these? Or, will we catechize with an eye toward the possible development of moral doctrine? Some pastoral leaders who hoped for this development during the last thirty years were led to advise parishioners to "follow their own conscience." Now those same pastoral leaders are faced with the troubling reality that many Catholics did just that, but without a concurrent development of Church doctrine to affirm the direction those consciences took. The massive disagreement between what is taught by the Church and what is held as morally true by much of the laity and many clerics on sexual issues, for example, has been well documented. Noted as well is the growing opposition within the Church to papal and episcopal teaching on issues such as capital punishment, assisted suicide, artificial reproduction, and prudential strategies for assisting the poor.

We believe a continuation of the individualism which fueled the philosophy of the autonomous conscience will do little to promote a Catholic ethos within parishes. In response to this individualism, and as a means to stop the fracturing of parishioners from

---

[1] William Bole, "Is America All Too Much With Us?" *Our Sunday Visitor* 86:1 (May 4, 1997): 9.

the truths of ecclesial teaching, some pastoral leaders have teetered toward authoritarianism and legalism in the liturgical and catechetical ministry. In this book we present an image of parish moral life that instead first emphasizes the necessity of converting one's heart to Christ in order to then appropriate a Catholic vision of what is good. Truly, the moral life is fueled by the community's devotion to Christ, because he alone is "the way, and the truth, and the life" (Jn 14:6). In this regard we affirm the calls by Paul VI and John Paul II for the re-evangelization of the Church. We also affirm that it is necessary to promote due respect for ecclesial tradition in the formation of people in the Catholic life. This respect is not to be understood as a blind obedience, which is beneath human dignity, but as a trust in the abiding presence of the Spirit in the moral teachings of the Church.

What is called for at this present time are pastoral leaders who can teach the skills of moral discernment. We need to educate parishioners to distinguish the voices of moral truth from those of propaganda, political ideology or personal bias. A focus on the discernment of moral truth is central to re-evangelization, but moral truth is to be embraced out of a character formed by loving the good in Christ. As Vincent MacNamara has stated:

"We need... to return from the self-centered concept of sincerity to the other-centered concept of truth. If we were wise enough and could only educate our desires we might find that living the truth is doing what we most want to do.... It is not easy. To be disposed to receive wisdom... is a conversion."[2]

Moral truth expresses itself in behavior that embodies what is good, as known through our Catholic identity and as personally appropriated by each individual believer in freedom and intelligence. Therefore, behavior, communal allegiance, and personal freedom all coalesce to create the moral person.

The time has come for pastoral leaders to help a new genera-

---

[2] Vincent MacNamara, "The Moral Journey," *The Way Supplement* 88 (Spring 1997): 11.

tion of Catholic parishioners embrace Catholicity amidst a secular culture that aims to reduce and measure our personal dignity by the market standards of production and consumption. Our dignity is not exhausted by market, political, or media definitions. Our dignity is not simply defined by "free choice." The goal of a parish — which has evangelization and a desire to love what is good at its heart — is to embody in its behavior, celebrate in its liturgies, and proclaim in its teachings that human dignity is preserved when one is related to Christ, his Church, and the moral truth.

The overarching question we are interested in is: How will our moral characters be formed as Catholic? In the first chapter we set the stage by presenting a picture of the current state of moral understanding in the parish. Can the parish become a community which actually has a role in the moral decisions of parishioners? Can pastoral leaders actually teach parishioners to discern right and wrong, instead of simply sending them away to be alone with their consciences or with an answer from a catechism? In other words, can the parish become a vibrant center for moral discernment? In becoming this center, we hope that pastoral leaders will reject a moral formation method which affirms either individualism or magisterial fundamentalism. In this book we are exploring what it means to abide with people as they deliberate about moral behavior.

In the second chapter we meditate on the heart of the parish: the Eucharist. In this worship celebration the identifying character of the Catholic is formed by the individual being configured with the community to Christ's life, death, and resurrection. Through the worship of God in the Eucharist, participants adhere to Christ and find within that communion an identity. This communion forms moral character through the virtues of devotion and adoration. The moral renewal of the parish hinges on the conscious participation of parishioners in the content of the Mass and the people's appropriation of its mysteries in Christian living. Ultimately, we need God's help to resist evil. We cannot settle for anything less than loving the Lord with our whole heart, soul, and strength, and our neighbor as ourselves (Mt 22:34-40). This resisting of evil and embracing of the good God is the heart of Christian morality, and a core meaning at the center of liturgical prayer.

The third chapter concretizes the first two by analyzing the scope and process of actual moral discernment. If pastoral leadership is not to leave parishioners alone in their discernment or prematurely cut off such deliberations with "answers," how then does being conformed to Christ's paschal mystery in the Eucharist affect our discernment of what is good and bad? Out of a mind formed by communal worship and the adoration of God comes an awareness that being in communion with God is central to ethical deliberation. Christian moral judgment is not simply "me making a decision for myself," but "me making a decision with Christ," who dwells within the conscience as Truth. Reason can see more when it is devoted to Christ and is not clouded by self-centeredness. Our moral reasonings are more reliable when informed by our loving participation in worship.[3] The virtuous character of individual believers which springs from worship is at the service of both ethical discernment and the moral education of the parish community.

The fourth and fifth chapters explicate some contemporary moral issues that parishioners currently face, such as the moral meaning of marriage, physician-assisted suicide, poverty, and the public role of the Catholic citizen. Amidst a culture which demands we attend to *its* values, our task is to encourage deliberation on these issues in light of our *Catholic* identity.

The last chapter contextualizes the moral questions of our time within the various events and small groups which may be present within a parish. In this we include the importance of preaching, evangelization, young adult formation and the reception of new Catholics into the Church. By doing this, we hope to give direction to those pastoral ministers laboring within these fields and small groups.

---

[3] See Roberta Bondi, *To Pray and to Love* (Minneapolis, MN: Fortress Press, 1991) 36.

In the end, we suggest that pastoral leaders should hone their skills as *experts in moral discernment* and abide with parishioners in compassion. Of course, the judgment of conscience is the ultimate subjective standard for making moral decisions; in its deliberations, however, the conscience should not be falsely cut off from the Catholic tradition in the name of exalting the individual or free choice. The parish stands as that most immediate expression of Catholic life and therefore holds a vital place, second to the family, as the community of faith formation. Through the spiritual life of the parishioner, the intellect develops under the influence of the affections, and moral behavior comes to embody that to which the mind lovingly attends. The Catholic parish exists to focus our hearts and minds upon what we love: God. It stands as that gathering of believers who pass on an identity transcending and embracing culture, class, gender, and all other particulars, as it explicitly grasps, expresses, and celebrates our ultimate identity as "friends of God." We hope this book will make readers think about recommitting themselves to the regeneration of a truly Catholic moral identity through the gathered community called the parish.

MORAL FORMATION IN THE PARISH

CHAPTER ONE

THE ECLIPSE OF THE PARISH

I. THE MORAL ATMOSPHERE IN THE CULTURE AND IN THE PARISH

We are living in a time that has made an intellectual movement — the Enlightenment — into a slogan seen widely on car-bumper stickers, "Question Authority." But this movement, which by and large can be lauded for the fruit it bore in contemporary society's respect for secular experience, is itself being questioned today. Contemporary theology asks if the Enlightenment's "un-fettered" mind, as opposed to a mind that attends to ecclesial sources, has led us to a better grasp of the human good. Without losing the vital advances of religious liberty and rightful secular autonomy, which had their seeds in the Enlightenment, it can be asked if the Church's conversation with society has broken down into nothing more than a shouting match between the causes of narrow interest groups. Does the conversation need to be re-grounded so that the dialogue between the authority of God's word, as mediated by the Church, and the rightfully autonomous and secular powers of culture and government can continue? In other words, has the balance shifted not only in favor of secular author-ity but also specifically *against* sources of faith? And alternately, can a Christian who sees little value in the *secular* truly be of a faith

1

that has the doctrine of the Incarnation near to its core? Nonetheless, the recognition that the world has a legitimate autonomy from the Church has a dark side as well. Dermot Lane suggests that "[There] is a growing realization that modernity itself is an ambiguous enterprise and that in many respects the inflated claims of modernity relating to the promise of progress, the promotion of endless growth and development have become bankrupt."[1]

In this type of intellectual atmosphere, which, to some extent, emphasizes being suspicious of authority, it might be good to be suspicious of suspicion and listen anew to the moral tradition of the Church, to allow ourselves to be questioned by it. Those who have questioned ecclesial authority over the last thirty years, those pastoral leaders and theologians on the partisan left and right, have themselves become the new authority structure in the popular Church and should be challenged by the questions found in doctrinal texts and in the witnessing texts of saintly lives.[2] Can Catholics spend some time allowing their lives to be challenged by the tradition as found in Scripture, doctrine, and the lives of the saints?[3] It is likely that some level of disagreement over Church teaching will be perennial. We believe, however, that Catholics need

---

[1] Dermot Lane, "Reclaiming Eschatology," *Josephinum Journal of Theology*, n.s. 1:2 (Summer /Fall 1994): 10.

[2] The tags "left" and "right" are notoriously slippery. By the "left" we mean those positions which have generally been noted to be politically liberal: support for democratization of the Church, universal or some legal access to physician-assisted suicide, abortion, artificial contraception, and approval of divorce and remarriage within the Church. By the "right" we refer to those positions which support capital punishment during the current ecclesial call to forego such state activity, absolute bans on abortion, artificial contraception, and minimum support, if any, for government welfare for the poor.

   We see the Church doctrine itself as appealingly paradoxical on these issues because as a whole it cannot be categorized as liberal or conservative, left or right. For example, to hold a Catholic position, one would have to be both against capital punishment and abortion. These two positions are not readily found in either those who claim to be liberal or conservative. The doctrine itself confounds these camps and engages them in a question about truth that is not inconsistent but enticingly paradoxical. These tags become less and less useful as one surveys the sweep of Catholic moral and social ethics.

[3] See Stephen E. Fowl and L. Gregory Jones, *Reading in Communion: Scripture and Ethics in Christian Life* (Grand Rapids: Eerdmans, 1991) 42.

to reassess how much of the disagreement is based on authentic rejection of the truth as known in Church doctrine, and how much is based on a lack of explicit moral education for adults compounded by the presence of politicized thinking from the left and the right. Can we recover the positive elements of Catholic morality, and present the moral life as the appropriation of what is good and not simply as obedience to law or an adventure in individualism and privacy?

A. Moral Discernment

Vatican Council II called for the renewal of moral theology.[4] Since then, many moral theologians have been searching for new ways to express and resolve the perennial problem of how people ought to discern right and wrong behavior according to a Christian understanding of the human person. This is the question of *method* in moral theology. Furthermore, some of these theologians have worked to develop a process of articulating the foundations and methods of virtue formation.[5] The question about appropriate methods of moral decision-making is vital for parish life because each parishioner must come to utilize a specific way of judging immoral behavior. Part of the role of pastoral leadership is to assist parishioners in understanding which methods are substantial enough to encompass all relevant facets of moral truth.

On the academic front, there appears to be intellectual gridlock regarding methods of moral discernment. There are two

---

[4] *Optatum Totius* (Decree on Priestly Formation) 16. *Vatican Council II: The Conciliar and Post Conciliar Documents*, ed. Austin Flannery (Wilmington: Scholarly Resources, 1975): "In like manner the other theological subjects should be renewed through a more vivid contact with the mystery of Christ and the history of salvation. Special care should be given to the perfecting of moral theology. Its scientific presentation should draw more fully on the teaching of Sacred Scripture and should throw light on the exalted vocation of the faithful in Christ and their obligation to bring forth fruit in charity for the life of the world."

[5] Joseph Kotva, *The Christian Case for Virtue Ethics* (Washington, DC: Georgetown University Press, 1996).

firm camps: revisionists and traditionalists. Each provides persuasive arguments and espouses positions and methodologies that can differ in degree. The main disagreement in the debate is over which circumstances should be included in an adequate description of the object of a moral choice. For example, the revisionists would argue that masturbation should be considered only an ontic evil, not a moral evil, until one has considered the intention and relevant circumstances that prompted such behavior.[6] The traditionalists would hold that masturbation is to be judged always morally wrong due to its solitary character, with no further circumstances being relevant.

The revisionists reject the notion of intrinsic evils apart from a full consideration of the concrete relevant circumstances and intention of the moral agent. The traditionalists hold that intrinsic evils can be ascertained through norms, before and separate from any consideration of the individual agent's circumstances. Of course, individual culpability must still be ascertained in each case. The revisionists condemn evil acts; yet the point for them is that such acts are condemned only once they are determined to be evil and that the required discernment cannot be achieved apart from the context of real, concrete situations and circumstances. The revisionists include the consequences and circumstances of an act in the process of judging whether that act is right or wrong. The revisionists judge an act to be right or wrong in virtue of its consequences and circumstances, they do not say that moral evil may be done for the sake of good consequences.[7] The traditionalists accept that some acts are intrinsically evil (e.g., killing innocent life), and sufficient circumstances are already included within their object to determine their moral nature.

---

[6] Ontic evil is a term used by revisionists to describe the lack of perfection inherent in some actions (e.g., in committed homosexual unions there lacks a reproductive meaning, and masturbation for use in artificial reproduction lacks a unitive meaning). They would argue that this lack of perfection can be tolerated if there is proportionate reason for doing so.

[7] See Gareth Moore, "Some Remarks on the use of Scripture in *Veritatis Splendor*," in Joseph Selling et al., eds., *The Splendor of Accuracy* (Grand Rapids, MI: Eerdmans, 1994) 95.

We cannot simplistically put the tension between these academic camps aside. Both groups raise real issues and answer questions with compelling responses. Some in the Church fear that revisionist theories will lead us astray, or naively hope that if everyone thought like the traditionalists our Church would be peaceful. These theories, however, only articulate methods of thinking which in themselves are more or less helpful.

These ethical methodologies have to be placed in their proper context, which includes an assessment of the way people *really* make decisions in everyday life. Instead of instilling fear over ethical theories, pastoral leaders might want to educate people in the power to discern the movements of the Spirit and to be docile to its wisdom, for "when God wishes to speak to a man, who can hinder him, what reasonings of exegete or theologian?"[8] This is not to suggest that oracles replace reasoned deliberation in faith regarding the moral truth of any one particular situation, but simply to emphasize the primacy of the judgment of conscience formed within the Church community.[9]

Genuinely listening to conscience, to the heart in the midst of the Church, is the perennial skill needed for Christians. It is too easy to engage in self-deception and utilize ethical methods to rationalize behavior that simply promotes self-interest. As Bernard Häring has written, "The main thrust of the new *Catechism* is surely not an external obedience, but a profound vision of the obedience of faith in its mystical dimension."[10] Formation in the skill of discerning the "voice of God" should become the key educative and formative goal of all moral education in the parish, particularly for adults.

---

[8] Servais Pinckaers, "The Use of Scripture and the Renewal of Moral Theology: The *Catechism* and *Veritatis Splendor*," *The Thomist* 59 (January 1995): 17.

[9] On attending to "the voice of God," see *Gaudium et Spes* (Pastoral Constitution on the Church in the Modern World) 16. *Vatican Council II: The Conciliar and Post Conciliar Documents*, ed. Austin Flannery (Wilmington: Scholarly Resources, 1975). See also John Paul II, *Veritatis Splendor* (The Splendor of Truth) (Vatican City: Libreria Editrice Vaticana, 1993) 29 & 58.

[10] In Michael Walsh, *Commentary on the Catechism* (Collegeville, MN: Liturgical Press, 1994) 360.

Before this kind of formation can happen, two myths about moral decision making must be dismantled. The first myth fosters a person's isolation from the Church, and the second fosters isolation from the self. This isolationism can be seen in how the two moral methodologies reviewed above have become popularized and reduced to a caricature. The traditionalists, as represented by Germain Grisez and William E. May, for example, are reduced to simply saying that the magisterium has all the answers: just obey and all will be fine. The revisionists, represented by Charles Curran and Richard McCormick, are understood to be saying, "just follow your 'conscience' and all will be fine." These two popular caricatures of what moral discernment is all about conspire to make moral discernment with a pastoral leader irrelevant. In the first caricature, a person does not need any guidance in decision making because one is simply given the "answer" found in the *Catechism*, for example. In the second caricature, one does not need any guidance because the answer is already within the person in the deliberations of conscience. Neither the revisionists nor the traditionalists promote exactly what these popular images advocate.

Nonetheless, it is these reductionist images in the minds of some Catholics that have assisted in making real pastoral guidance in the area of morality pointless. In the "conscience" caricature, the ecclesial community and its leaders are extraneous to discernment, and in the "answer man" caricature the individual agent is irrelevant to moral decision making. Neither approach will do if we are to give respect to both the individual and the ecclesial community within which Catholics are morally formed.

B. *Parish Moral Atmosphere*

Somewhere between the Council's call for renewal and the theologians' interpretations of the meaning of that call, the role of the parish in moral formation has become obscured in three important ways. First, the conversation about renewing moral theology led many laypersons to mistranslate the meaning of conscience and its formation as something akin to a simple extension of American individualism[11] — which asserts, on a practical level, that one's sincerity of feeling in the "the heart" is the measure of sound moral judgment. Of course, attending to one's feelings has a role in moral formation and judgment, but it is not sufficient unto itself.[12]

The second mistranslation was to reduce moral questions simply to questions of authority and obedience. Obedience to authority is vital to moral formation but, as with feelings, it cannot carry the entire weight of how a Catholic chooses the good. This reductionist concept of obedience, or "blind" obedience to authority, was rejected by the Second Vatican Council when it promoted a dynamic, personal vision of decision making:

> For God willed that man should "be left in the hand of his own counsel" so that he might of his own accord seek his Creator and freely attain his full and blessed perfection by cleaving to him. Man's dignity therefore requires him to act out of conscious and free choice, as moved and drawn in a personal way from within, and not by blind impulses in himself or by mere external constraint.[13]

If one embraced a blindly obedient model of Christian ethics, God would have no real agent to call to the good; God would simply be play-acting at relationships outside of the Trinity. This extreme vision of the moral life as obedience alone does not have very many adherents (at least not many who will admit it governs their choices); rather, this kind of thinking works most powerfully as a hidden standard in the minds of some who fear the dissolution of Catholic moral identity, and the rise of a Church of isolated indi-

---

[11] See Robert Bellah et al., *Habits of the Heart: Individualism and Commitment in American Life* (Berkeley, CA: University of California Press, 1985). Harold Bloom, *The American Religion* (NY: Simon & Schuster, 1992).

[12] See G. Simon Harak, *Virtuous Passions: The Formation of Christian Character* (New York: Paulist Press, 1993).

[13] *Gaudium et Spes* 17.

viduals, each claiming moral autonomy from the tradition. To have this apprehension of autonomous decision making, in itself, is not off the mark, and in fact may show some insight. A legitimate aversion to individualism in moral decision making, however, should not lead one to an authoritarian promotion of blind obedience. There is an essential role for obedience in the moral life and for pastoral moral formation. Part of our goal in this book is to recover the positive and life-giving characteristics of obedience.

A third component that has obscured the role of the parish in moral formation is the seeming reluctance on the part of some pastoral leaders to raise controversial moral issues in homilies, seminars, or adult education programs within the parish. Of course, it is not a matter of simply raising issues but of equipping parishioners with the spiritual and intellectual tools needed to make sound choices about moral issues. This unofficial conspiracy of silence is most damaging to the role parishes should play in moral formation because it compounds an already common notion in society that religion is irrelevant to public life.

Thus, in the last thirty years since the Council, there has developed a continuum along which one might discover the stance of the Catholic parishioner toward the moral life: autonomous individualism, on the one hand, mistakenly understood to be a life of following one's "conscience"; and, on the other hand, the fearful reaction to this mistake by some pastoral leaders who promote obedience to authority as the only way to "fix the present anarchy." Finally, this fear of moral anarchy and the cultural resistance which meets many of the Church's moral teachings has led to the unofficial conspiracy of silence at the parish level.

C. *Spirituality and Morality: A Key to Parish Moral Renewal*

Gradations of autonomy, fear of anarchy, and silence have ruled the day for too long in the parish, and so the Church needs *positive* explorations into the moral life. The Catholic parish can become a vehicle for these explorations if its leaders and parishio-

ners come to see the parish as a place of basic conscience formation. The key to this revival of the parish as a center of moral formation is to be found in explicitly linking moral formation of the
conscience with Christian spirituality. By doing so the pastoral
leader invites parishioners into a relationship of love with God. It
is from within this devotion to God that the conscience is claimed
by the moral truth and hence judges the good out of love for Goodness itself. The Council itself hinted at a unity between morality
and spirituality when it said,

> For God willed that man should be left in the hand of
> his own counsel so that he might of his own accord seek
> his Creator… by cleaving to him…. It is only by the
> help of God's grace that man can give his actions their
> full and proper relationship to God.[14]

In other words, we are to be left to our own counsel so that
we might take counsel from God. In this paradoxical principle is
the key to a characteristically Christian moral life. We are not alone
in our moral deliberations, nor are we given the answers by some
supernatural circumvention of the intellect and affections. Rather,
we recognize the moral truth by "cleaving" to God. The word
"cleave" in Latin can also be rendered "inhere," or "belong." And
so, if we want to be free, to be left in the hand of our own counsel,
we recognize that this freedom can only be accomplished if it is
ordered to our love of God.[15] If we belong to Christ we will know
with Christ, in the Spirit, what is right and good. Our relationship with God in Christ is involved in the very essence of what it
means to choose the good in freedom. As John Paul II said in his
recent encyclical *Veritatis Splendor:*

---

[14] *Gaudium et Spes* 17.
[15] See Paul J. Wadell, *Friendship and the Moral Life* (Notre Dame, IN: University of
Notre Dame Press, 1989); *Friends of God: Virtues and Gifts in Aquinas* (New York:
P. Lang, 1991); *The Primacy of Love: An Introduction to the Ethics of Thomas Aquinas*
(New York: Paulist Press, 1992).

Moral conscience does not close man within an insur-
mountable and impenetrable solitude, but opens him
to the call, to the voice of God. In this, and not in anything else, lies the entire mystery and the dignity of the
moral conscience: in being the place, the sacred place
where God speaks to man.[16]

When it comes to the formation of conscience, the Catholic
parish is not the place to simply repeat the cultural values of
America, or the latest theories from popular theologians; nor is it
the place to "lay down the law" according to the magisterium, exclusively. The parish, however, is the place where one can be invited to *discern* the moral truth and thus live the good life in Christ,
renewing not only self and parish, but also the culture.[17] By explicitly linking love of the good with love of God, the parish draws
from the strength of its rightful mission: a community that fosters
character formation and *true devotion*. The heart of parish moral
renewal will be to let people hear (word), see (witness), and live
(worship)[18] the truths found within our Catholic moral heritage.
In faith, the truth will bind parishioners because they have confidence in the Spirit who leads them into all that is real, all that is
"of God." Spiritual renewal and moral renewal cannot be separated.
Moral formation and loving devotion to God interpenetrate. This
confidence in the Spirit is instilled through efforts at re-evangelization, which we shall discuss below.

---

[16] *Veritatis Splendor* 58.

[17] John Paul II, *Evangelium Vitae* (The Gospel of Life) (Vatican City: Libreria Editrice
Vaticana, 1995) 95.

[18] See Michael Skelley, *The Liturgy of the World: Karl Rahner's Theology of Worship*
(Minneapolis, MN: Liturgical Press, 1991). "Rahner is convinced that the liturgy
will become a life-giving encounter with absolute Mystery only if we first discover
the experience of God hidden in the midst of our daily lives" (p. 75). See also Anthony Ciorra, *Everyday Mysticism: Cherishing the Holy* (New York: Crossroad, 1995).

D. *Reason: Its Power and Its Limits*

The Catholic tradition has great confidence that truth as embodied in communal practices and doctrine will invite and persuade people to moral conversion. The Catholic vision of the moral life is one which sees moral deliberation (natural law) as opening up to the wisdom of God. Catholics are not afraid of a good argument. This explains, in part, why our tradition has welcomed schools, colleges, and universities as vital facets of the faith community. The truth, if given a fair hearing and time, will win the day. If this search for the moral truth is linked with prayer, fasting, and other practices and devotions, Catholics believe that God will speak to the community through its leaders and from within the consciences of its members.

This hopeful vision of the function of reason is not to disregard the real presence of sin and evil among us. We are all well aware of evil clouding our minds in self-deception. That which appears to be truth can in fact be egoism rationalized. My "agenda" can be imposed on others as if it were the word of God. Out of deep respect for the power of evil one ought to embrace the call to explicitly form parishioners in moral truth and to do so imbued with a Christian spirituality. Only by the disciplines and devotions of a genuine Christian spirituality can we face evil and have that encounter transformed into conversion.[19] By Christian spirituality we mean those attitudes and ecclesial practices (worship, prayer, virtues, etc.) that seek to facilitate union with God in Christ through the Holy Spirit.

In raising ethical issues within a parish setting, pastoral leaders would be wise to brace themselves for a confrontation with evil. Most likely, evil will appear as "hardness of heart" within those who are afraid to change behavior, or even perhaps within other pastoral leaders who might not want to face years of rationalizing and

---

[19] Mark O'Keefe, O.S.B., *Becoming Good, Becoming Holy: On the Relationship of Christian Ethics and Spirituality* (New York: Paulist, 1995) 35-37.

excuses for lapses in their own teaching, preaching, or behavior. To even begin a pastoral moral renewal within one's parish, the leadership must take evil seriously. Before any public educational events are undertaken in the parish as a whole, parish leaders should enter a time of personal, spiritual, and moral formation. If this preparation is not undertaken, resistance to the moral renewal process on the part of some parishioners might catch leaders unaware. If resistance is encountered, the leadership team does not want to lose heart and give up the planned renewal, but rather remain hopeful that in time the Spirit will guide leaders and people to the good. Despite the reality of people closing their hearts, our tradition believes that reason, imbued with the love of God, can come to grasp what is good for us. Moral formation and development is ultimately a hopeful ministry, and looks forward to sinners repenting and enjoying the peace known in faithfully living their human vocation as a Christian.

II. HOW TO READY PERSONS, PARISHES, AND PASTORS FOR MORAL RENEWAL

A. Alter Practices that Keep Us from Focusing on God

How do we ready people for moral conversion? In order to call for moral renewal, one has to change any practice that facilitates an exclusive focus upon secular experience to the detriment of being open to God. This purifying is in truth a cleansing, not a destroying, because God is mediated through secular experience as well. This purifying, which will prepare individuals and the parish for moral renewal, is not an otherworldly longing but a fuller vision of what counts as reality in *this* world. And to believers, what counts as reality in their world vision includes a sense of the community's relatedness to God. In Christian churches, the call to re-think how far we have distanced ourselves from God — in our joy over embracing the secular — falls under the heading of re-evangelization. The pope is succinct in his description of some current ecclesial and cultural postures. Re-evangelization is necessary, says Pope John Paul II, when Christians live "as if God did not exist.... There is no longer a need to fight against God; the individual feels he is simply able to live without him."[20]

We live in a sort of mindless ingestion of "the current." Combine this attitude with indifference to religion, or even more sadly, "living as if God didn't exist," and we end up with very little in the ecclesial world counting as reality. Of course, God is bigger than the Church, understood in its institutional operation. God is among us, calling us to holiness through the everyday activities of family, work and recreation. This graced presence, however, can go unnoticed and/or unheeded, and so the parish beckons as a gathering of people who help to point explicitly to the presence of God in the ordinary.[21]

Within this environment of cultural indifference to God and preoccupation with secular experience comes the teaching of the Church through three new documents: the *Catechism*, *Veritatis Splendor* and *Evangelium Vitae*.[22] In summary and broadly con-

---

[20] Pope John Paul II, *Pastores Dabo Vobis* (I Will Give You Shepherds: On the Formation of Priests in the Circumstances of the Present) (Washington, DC: United States Catholic Conference, 1992) 7 & 8.

[21] See Carolyn Thomas, *Gift and Response: A Biblical Spirituality for Contemporary Christians* (Mahwah, NJ: Paulist Press, 1994).

[22] There are many good studies of these documents in print. Our purpose is not to rehearse the content of the *Catechism*, *Veritatis Splendor* and *Evangelium Vitae*; rather, we wish to emphasize those aspects of these documents that can offer direction for pastoral moral renewal. See Cardinal Joseph Ratzinger, *Introduction to the Catechism of the Catholic Church* (San Francisco: Ignatius Press, 1994); Thomas Reese, ed., *The Universal Catechism Reader* (San Francisco: Harper & Row, 1990); Selling et. al., *The Splendor of Accuracy*; and Michael E. Allsopp and John J. O'Keefe, eds., *Veritatis Splendor: American Responses* (Kansas City, MO: Sheed & Ward, 1995). Another excellent biblically based introduction to practical moral theology which makes considerable use of the *Catechism*, *Veritatis Splendor* and *Evangelium Vitae* is the recent work of Benedict Ashley, O.P., *Living the Truth in Love* (New York: Alba House, 1996).

strued, these documents can be seen as a response to our weariness over simply reflecting upon secular experience — particularly as manifested in self-interest and "special interest" groups — and with our indifference to or muting of the sacred.

B. Humility and Listening

The society's emphasis on the secular, on "my needs," on "power," and on "my rights" has been one-sidedly promoted to the neglect of respect for the sacred, listening, and humility. Even in raising these last two traits of humility and listening, we are conscious that very powerful figures in history have utilized these virtues to their gain and to the detriment of the poor. In other words, it is very easy to oppress people who simply listen, cooperate, and "know their place." We address these words to Catholic pastoral leaders in the Western world, most of whom, however, come from privilege simply by virtue of their education. In this book, it is to them that discussion of these virtues, properly understood, is addressed. Parishioners look to pastoral leaders for examples of lives lived in radical dependency not upon the self and one's own powers, but upon God. We ask ourselves, to whom have pastoral leaders been listening? And, before what or whom have pastoral leaders been humbled?

Humility and listening are virtues necessary for religion, and stand opposed to a self-centered vision of ministry. The most creative act of any human person occurred under the banner of raptly listening to God: Mary's *fiat* to the angel. From that kind of listening flowed the salvation of the world. Creativity and power are best contextualized in a relationship with the divine, not some will to power or glorification of one's own native talents. At the same time, pastoral ministers certainly ought not be about the business of having people "obey" in a narrow sense of that term. Recent history shows that they will not, nor should they. But can we have persons "listen" for the truth in Church teaching and be attracted by that truth and choose accordingly? Can we help people see that truths are expressed in the moral doctrines of the Church, and that doctrine is not depleted of relevance for contemporary parishioners?

In the context of forming parishioners and pastoral leaders in the virtues of listening and humility we have hope that the parish can become a center of moral discernment.[23] It can be a place of open conversation, guided by Catholic moral tradition, on the moral questions of our day. If the parish does not become this place of discernment, a community that distinguishes right from wrong, we leave Catholics no alternative but to seek moral formation elsewhere. How odd and unfortunate that for some Catholics the parish is the last place they would think of going to get assistance in discerning the good.

C. Establish Trust, Seek Forgiveness and Reconciliation

If a portion of a parish's mission is to facilitate moral discernment within its members, then trust needs to be in place — pastoral leadership needs to build trust between itself and the laity. Processes need to be developed, strengthened, or affirmed by which laity can communicate with clergy or pastoral leadership. The fear of being "shut out" by the clergy is still present in some laity. This has its complement in the fear some clergy experience toward the still growing independent nature of many lay persons. The easing of tensions between some laity and some clergy remains an urgent moral need in parishes throughout the nation. Without mutual trust no real moral renewal can be implemented.

This tension between laity and clergy is part of a wider cultural vision in America that rejects hierarchical leadership as elitist, and looks for more democratic ruling structures within

---

[23] See James Keating, "The Good Life: An Invitation to Holiness," *Church* 11 (Summer 1995): 15-20. See also Joan Mueller, *Faithful Listening: Discernment in Everyday Life* (Kansas City, MO: Sheed & Ward, 1996).

churches. Compound this unease over hierarchical ruling models with the media's exposure of sexual and economic sins of clergy, and pastoral leadership finds itself in a difficult environment within which to call people to moral renewal.

An essential component of (re)establishing moral authority for clergy and pastoral leadership will be for them to first seek forgiveness and reconciliation where needed. On the international stage, Pope John Paul II has been exemplary in this regard by publicly asking for forgiveness from Protestants, Jews, and women, among others.[24] Pastors can take courage from the example of the pope, and where appropriate ask for forgiveness regarding their actions or attitudes (e.g., being too authoritarian, for pastoring out of fear not faith, putting too much emphasis on material things, being sexist, having a poor management style, etc.). The key point here is the necessity to re-establish contact with the people through an open heart, showing the people that their leaders are serious about moral renewal and wish to lead them to conversion. Reestablishing trust is the vital beginning point.

On their part, the laity are called to forgive their leaders and incorporate any inflicted wounds into their love for Christ and the Church. Of course this healing process is not simple, but it is essential to the health of the parish. The healing process will be facilitated if Catholics have an open, docile heart regarding moral doctrine. When pastoral leadership teaches Catholic ethics, do the laity earnestly seek the Spirit in such teaching or simply abide by their previous judgments made in different situations and possibly for motives other than fidelity to one's baptismal identity?

Two other dispositions might facilitate moral renewal if they take root or are strengthened in pastoral leadership. First among these qualities would be a love for the people of the parish. By this

---

[24] Luigi Accattoli, *When a Pope Asks Forgiveness: The Mea Culpa's of John Paul II*, tr. Jordan Aumann, O.P. (New York: Alba House, 1998); also Susan Hines, "Pope Asks Forgiveness for the Church's Past Sins," *St. Anthony Messenger* 103 (July 1995): 7. See also John Paul II, *Mulieris Dignitatem* (On the Dignity and Vocation of Women). Apostolic Letter, August 15, 1988. See *Origins* 18 (October 3, 1988): 261+.

we mean that pastors have the best spiritual interests of the parishioners in mind within the context of ministry. Due to the politicizing of ethics (i.e., conservative, liberal), it is "fashionable" in some circles today to vilify those with whom one disagrees on current issues. It is important to remember that ethics has become so politicized that in some minds "liberal" and "conservative" have become equivalent to morally right or wrong, each characterized according to which political camp one happens to inhabit. Any partisan allegiances that will set a pastoral leader against any one parishioner ought to be consumed in the love the Spirit wants to give pastors for all their parishioners. John Paul II reminds us, "The missionary is a person of charity. In order to proclaim to all his [or her] brothers and sisters that they are loved by God and are capable of loving, he [or she] must show love towards all… without exclusion or partiality."[25]

Second, the pastor or pastoral leader must be led by the Spirit. In order to oversee the moral renewal of the parish the pastoral leader "lives a life of complete docility to the Spirit…. This docility then commits us to receive the gifts of fortitude and discernment, which are essential elements of missionary spirituality."[26] Only loving, courageous, and discerning leaders will not grow faint at the resistance that possibly awaits them in the task of assisting people to confront their own personal cooperation with evil. As Christ taught his disciples in confronting evil, "This kind (of evil, of demon) cannot be driven out by anything but prayer" (Mk 9:29; Mt 17:21).

In order to expedite moral renewal during this present time of considerable moral disagreement within the Church, it is necessary to turn explicitly to the Holy Spirit, not with a pre-established agenda, but simply with open hearts and hands. Pastoral leaders will want to come before the people not simply with answers to moral questions but with pathways to soften hardened

---

[25] John Paul II, *Redemptoris Missio* (On the Permanent Validity of the Church's Missionary Mandate) (Washington, DC: United States Catholic Conference, 1990) 89.

[26] *Redemptoris Missio* 87.

hearts. The "answers" have been rejected by a significant number of people. Pastors may want to set time aside to search with parishioners for the moral truth. In doing so, pastors will be saying in all honesty, "Some dissent, some do not; let's search together in prayer, in humility and with sincere and open hearts for what Christ is calling this parish to do in the moral life."

D. Specific Ways to Prepare for Moral Conversion

1. Looking to Jesus

Obviously not everyone will respond favorably to an explicit parish moral renewal process. But consciously developing parish moral formation around moral goods will stimulate conversion. In *Veritatis Splendor* the pope gives us the key to moral revival in our parishes. He invites conversion and gives primacy to love over commands and rules. The pope quotes St. Augustine, "But who can doubt that love comes first? For the one who does not love has no reason for keeping the commandments."[27] In this fashion blind obedience is rejected by the pope: "Human dignity requires man to act through conscious and free choice, as motivated and prompted personally from within, and not through blind internal impulse or merely external pressure."[28] God is said to care for us from "within" through our loving search for the truth.[29] When addressing the bishops the pope points to the correct disposition needed in the pastoral renewal of moral living.

> Dear Brothers in the Episcopate, we must not be content to merely warn the faithful about the errors and dangers of certain ethical theories. We must first of all show the inviting splendor of that truth which is Jesus

---

[27] *Veritatis Splendor* 22.
[28] *Veritatis Splendor* 42.
[29] *Veritatis Splendor* 43.

Christ himself. In him who is Truth (Jn 14:16) man can understand fully… his vocation to freedom in obedience to the divine law summarized in the commandment to love God and neighbor.[30]

Conversion away from sin and toward Christ is the heart of Christian moral living. "The secret of the Church's educative power [is] not so much in doctrinal statements and pastoral appeals to vigilance, as in *constantly looking to the Lord Jesus.*"[31] But did not parishes have the "catechism of love" throughout the 1970's?[32] As a result of emphasizing love rather than obedience to moral truths, parish religious education during the 1970's yielded less knowledge about what behaviors are right and wrong than did previous religious education efforts. But positively, the spirit of the '70's spawned great movements of people who fell in love with Jesus (e.g., Cursillo, Charismatic Renewal, Emmaus, TEC, Marriage Encounter, etc.). Today we are no longer surprised as we travel throughout the country to note that a significant number of people working in Church ministry, and witnessing to Christ in the secular world, were formed in one of those movements noted above. What we need now is both universal revival of *authentic teaching* (the *Catechism* at least has this content, but it has to be expressed through sound catechetical methods) linked with the *spirit of conversion* that God unleashed in the Church during the 1970's and is doing so always. As a result of "falling in love" with Christ, the disciple responds to His voice in the conscience, and is oriented toward what is good.

---

[30] *Veritatis Splendor* 83.

[31] *Veritatis Splendor* 85.

[32] This was the era of such books as Thomas A. Harris' *I'm O.K., You're O.K.* (New York: Avon, 1973). These books represented the thinking of the decade wherein much behavior, which traditionally would have been called sin, was accepted in the name of non-judgmental acceptance of persons.

2. Prayer

What is needed to begin a serious moral renewal can be simply stated: the listening hearts and minds of pastoral leadership and the people. Any moral renewal will fail without prayer. Without prayerful hearts an organized effort at renewal may, in fact, simply stiffen the positions of those who already disagree with the Church's moral doctrine, or cement the "obedient" in self-righteousness. Only prayer can break through to the truth, exposing our blind spots, pet causes, and comfortable sloganeering.[33]

Prayer is also needed to instill resolve, since any attempt at honest communication on moral issues may become volatile due to years of anger, betrayal of trust, hypocrisy and the rationalizing of our sinful behaviors. We need to discern prudently and pray about which parish forums to utilize for listening and teaching. Since the moral life touches the human identity so deeply, some are likely to be defensive in the initial discussions about moral behavior; some will be silent; and, most sadly, some will not participate at all because of "hardness of heart." The tone of any parish renewal process should be one of healing. The process should embody a spiritual cry for moral fidelity and authenticity, not a frustrated grimace by an angry parent. Resolving moral discord through authoritarian crackdowns will simply invite parishioners to dismiss the pastor as irrelevant, and, what is worse, he will be distorting the *splendor* of the moral truth into the *commands* of the moral truth. The laws are not compelling in and of themselves, but the truth they aim to convey is. It is *the good* that attracts the conscience, not norms, *per se*. We need to listen as God speaks to our hearts through the Church's ministry of sacrament, word, service, doctrine, and piety.

One possible reason that positive approaches to the moral life have not achieved a more proportionate level of "unity in difference" since the Second Vatican Council might be due to a lack of intentional, explicit openness on the part of parishes to come be-

---

[33] *Veritatis Splendor* 88.

fore God on this matter of moral formation. Pastoral moral formation is all too often only implied and, therefore, moral conversion is not fully embraced as a ministerial goal. Evidence of a disproportionate level of doctrinal disagreement can be seen by noting the failure of bishops to persuade Catholics and Americans in general to accept their position on any number of moral issues, such as: abortion, affirmative action, pre-marital sex, capital punishment, legalization of assisted suicide, government assistance for illegal and legal immigrants, etc.[34] One way to seek a coherence between popular opinion and pastoral persuasion is to promote communally-imbedded consciences and their formation within the parish.

3. The Importance of the Question, "Who?": The Dignity of Catholic Identity

Some might raise a caution here: "Wasn't placing conscience at the center of morality one of the initial problems which encouraged the rising permissiveness within our Church?" We answer that if the move to make conscience central to moral formation was a factor in the growth of subjectivist methods within some Catholic decision making, it was due to a faulty understanding of conscience. Popularly, conscience was interpreted within a context that exalted privacy and individualism rather than within an ecclesial context of prayerful obedience.[35] Conscience does not merely apply norms, but grasps the good that has to be done by me individually, and integrates the personal love of God with the search for truth.[36] Unsettling as it is, Catholic Americans ought to hear that conscience is not simply the isolated individual discerning the right, but rather the individual as member of the Church listening to the voice of God in his or her heart. Conscience opens one to the divine voice

---

[34] See James Keating, "Bias, Fear, and the Social Teachings of the Catholic Church," *Emmanuel* 101 (July-August, 1995): 342-350.

[35] *Catechism of the Catholic Church* (Vatican City: Libreria Editrice Vaticana, 1994) 1783-1785.

[36] *Catechism* 1783. Karl Rahner, "On the Question of a Formal Existential Ethics," *Theological Investigations*, vol. 2 (New York: Crossroad, 1990) 229.

— it does not shut the person up in the self.[37] What change in consciousness is needed to foster this communal sense of conscience?

a. A key contributor to today's anemic Catholic consciences is the lack of a sense of belonging to both the parish and the universal Church. For example, why would one want to listen to God within a conscience formed by a Church understood to be "a group of bishops and priests," or "a building," or "gathered strangers"? Moral renewal is supported when a parish gradually reclaims an authentic sense of Catholic identity.

The Catholic moral tradition, as seen in the *Catechism*'s structure as a whole, reflects the age-old insight that before one can do right behavior he or she must ground discernment of that behavior in a properly understood identity.[38] This attitude is summarized in St. Leo the Great's exclamation, "Christian remember your dignity."[39] This consciousness of one's own and others' dignity can be an aid in the process of moral formation and should contribute to a positive ecclesial context for discussing moral issues in a pastoral setting.

b. In America today many people begin to defend their moral actions by answering the question, "Why?" We have reduced the moral question simply to one of motive. Other legitimate aspects of the moral act, such as consequences, circumstances, and how the act impacts on the formation of personal virtue, are muted. We frequently hear people reasoning that, for instance, it is good to ask for physician-assisted suicide out of "concern" or love for my family and to "relieve their burdens." These are certainly noble motives, but the motive alone does not make an act good; motives do not in themselves designate an act to be virtuous. "Why?" is an essential question in any moral analysis, but it is not sufficient.

In light of the Church's teaching on human dignity, and the noted weaknesses in some people's understanding of what a parish community is, the primary question one ought to ask in dis-

---

[37] *Veritatis Splendor* 58.
[38] *Catechism* 1700-1715.
[39] *Catechism* 1691.

cerning moral behavior is not "Why?" but "Who?"[40] Who is performing this act, and/or with whom or toward whom is one acting? This kind of questioning allows the agent to name and "see"
the person affected by his or her actions: this is my neighbor, a
stranger, a spouse of another, my spouse, a baby, etc. Awareness
of one's baptismal identity can further contextualize our moral
deliberation by eliciting the next logical question: In light of the
faith, in this situation, and under these circumstances, how ought
one treat self, baby, spouse, another person's spouse, stranger, or
neighbor?

This way of thinking sets up a positive construct for moral
analysis because it frames the moral question in the context of the
goodness of persons and their dignity. Ultimately, morality is about
the good, not law; and the penultimate good is the human person. But, first, parishioners should be clear about who they really
are in baptism and the importance that *identity* makes to their ethical discernment.[41]

4. Fear and the Loss of Catholic Identity

Despite some clear evidence that some facets of our culture
disdain the virtues of Christian morality, the Church ought not
be driven by fear in its efforts at moral renewal. Parishes are part
of the society and should not become stationary Noah's Arks
wherein pastors close the door and doom the rest of culture to
oblivion. If moral disintegration is real in our society, and sectar-

---

[40] Kenneth R. Melchin, "Moral Decision-Making and the Role of the Moral Question," *Method: Journal of Lonergan Studies* 11 (1993): 215-228.

[41] "It would be a very serious error to conclude... that the Church's teaching is essentially only an ideal which must then be adapted, proportioned and graduated to the
so-called concrete possibilities of man.... But what are the concrete possibilities of
man? And of which man are we speaking? Of man dominated by lust or of man
redeemed by Christ?" (*Veritatis Splendor* 103).

    This is a vital paragraph for understanding the Pope's vision of the reality of moral
conversion. We can become good because in baptism our selfishness is conquered
in the grace of Christ. This is the identity of the Christian, the one who, with Christ,
in Christ, can conquer evil with good. This is true not strictly because of what one
does, but because of who one is.

ian living is not an option for Catholics, then perhaps we need to
bring the parish on "retreat" in order to refocus our formation
explicitly on moral renewal. By using the word "retreat" we are
simply referring to an organizing symbol for some kind of explicit
process or educational event(s) that can assist parishioners to take
a hard look at how a public Catholic presence in American society
can be strengthened by moral renewal within our own communities.

The *Catechism*, as well as *Veritatis Splendor* and *Evangelium
Vitae*, can be used as the building blocks of this "retreat" for parish moral renewal. Most parishes do not have to start from ground
zero in any renewal process. Nonetheless, it is not surprising to find
some Catholics who have little or no cognizance of their moral
heritage. Some form of moral evangelization is needed for these
kinds of parishioners. As Servais Pinckaers notes, if we evangelize
the people and introduce them to the love of Christ through word,
sacrament, ministry, and piety, their hearts will open and be available to hear appeals from pastoral leaders regarding the truth of
moral living.[42]

What secures the moral life is a personal act of giving oneself
to God — the fruit of evangelization. As Paul said in Romans 12:1,

> I urge [or appeal to] you, therefore, brothers, by the
> mercy of God, to offer yourself [body] as a living sacri-
> fice, holy, and pleasing to God.... Do not conform
> yourself to this age but be transformed by the renewal
> of your mind, that you may discern what is the will of
> God, what is good, and pleasing and perfect.

In the giving of the self to God one can discern the good because
the mind has been renewed and is no longer simply a product of
the current age and culture. Pinckaers notes further that pastoral

---

[42] Servais Pinckaers, *The Sources of Christian Ethics* (Washington, DC: Catholic University of America Press, 1995) 12-13.

leaders should see no need to issue commands or orders as they would to servants, "for [the people of God] have opened their hearts to love; [the pastor] exhorts them by word and example, as brothers and sisters in Christ."[43] Commands are for slaves, not brothers and sisters.

The use of the *Catechism* and the papal encyclicals can only bear fruit if their wisdom is ordered toward the love of God and the good of parishioners. Use of these documents cannot be productively ordered to anxiety and fear over a loss of pastoral influence regarding what Catholics think ethically. Fear can be a signal, however, that something precious is being threatened, and in this way can be the initial indicator that some of the Catholic moral heritage is in danger of being undermined.[44] Nevertheless, fear cannot be the abiding affective power in any moral renewal — fear must be replaced by a love for the good and for parishioners. If the minister's fear remains the abiding affective power in parish renewal, it will simply make everyone involved defensive, and move some people to clutch more tightly to norms, laws, and precepts.

The *Catechism* and the papal encyclicals are gifts to the Church. And yet, some have already looked upon them as opportunities to assuage these fears of losing control. We do not believe this kind of attitude corresponds to the intent of these documents. Of course, the *Catechism* contains clear statements of moral doctrine, but that alone will not convert people who have disagreed with moral doctrine for many years. These clearly expressed norms cannot end our problems of the heart. Neither will these clearly expressed words mask the anxiety and fear with which some may deliver them. As Matthew's Gospel reminds us, "Fear is useless, what is needed is trust" (Mt 5:36). And furthermore, as Catholic moral tradition has long held, moral obligations are necessary, but they must be ordered to charity. To move the people of the parish

---

[43] Pinckaers, *Sources* 12.
[44] Sidney Callahan, *In Good Conscience* (New York: Harper, 1991) 24ff.

toward a reappropriation of their faith in God is the perennial task of securing a Catholic identity — an identity that bears fruit in courageous ethical decisions based on trust in God.

E. The Context of Renewal: A New Evangelization

The moral renewal of the parish can be fruitfully placed in the context of what some are calling the "new evangelization."[45] This form of evangelization recognizes the cultural influences of current society, which denigrate or weaken once vigorous Christian identities and values. The new evangelization is directed toward populations that "were Christianized in the past but are now living in a secularized world that denies religion any value and simply tolerates a private religion."[46] The new evangelization is directed to nominal Christians whose faith lacks roots, who in the name of freedom from authority rejected religion, or who, out of being abused by religious authority, rejected religion. Others in need of the new evangelization might simply have let their faith lie dormant under a flood of secular, familial, or professional interests. As Herve Carrier noted:

> When a second evangelization becomes necessary... there is no longer a supporting culture.... [I]t is opposed to the Church... or indifferent.... The tragedy of religious indifference is that the Gospel is neither completely unknown nor completely new.... Faith is both present and absent from the minds of the people.[47]

And again, as the pope wrote, a new evangelization is necessary in a time when Christians live "as if God did not exist.... There is no

---

[45] Herve Carrier, "Evangelization," *Dictionary of Fundamental Theology,* ed. Rene Latourelle and Rino Fisichella (New York: Crossroad, 1994) 287ff.

[46] Carrier 287.

[47] Carrier 289.

longer a need to fight against God; the individual feels he is simply able to do without him."[48]

The *Catechism* wants us to understand the commands of God in the context of a life freed from the slavery of sin.[49] Ultimately the moral life is a positive good to be embraced in a relationship with God in Christ. It is a burden which is light. The commands of moral living try to capture what life is like for those who belong to God. The section on moral living in the *Catechism* is called "life in Christ" (part three). And so, one can see that the *Catechism*'s vision of moral living is intimately connected to evangelization rather than law. What we want to bring before the people is the Church's vision of the adventure of holiness: a life of full collaboration between God's grace and human freedom. This is a profound trust in the renewing Spirit of God without losing the real tension of our sinful, limited nature. This is the Church speaking out of hope not naiveté.

Moral formation is a process of growth, a response to Christ as his disciple.[50] It emerges from a deepening consciousness of being profoundly loved by Christ. "Moral theology… takes into account first and foremost the spiritual dimension of the human heart and its vocation to divine love."[51] The paschal mystery of Christ stands as the paradigm for all that humans can achieve in God. From the incarnation with its joys of living ordinary lives of love, through the crucifixion as it tests our fidelity to that love and goodness, to the resurrection as that way of living which overflows in commitment transformed into steady wisdom, it is the grace of Christ in his paschal mystery which guides our hope in the moral life.[52]

---

[48] *Pastores Dabo Vobis* 7 & 8.

[49] *Catechism* 2057.

[50] *Catechism* 2234.

[51] *Veritatis Splendor* 112.

[52] See Daniel Stollenwerk, "Incarnation, Crucifixion, and Resurrection as Symbols of Life Events," *Josephinum Journal of Theology*, n.s. 2:2 (Summer/Fall 1995): 60-68.

Part of what happened to weaken moral consensus within the Church over the last thirty years is the influence of individualism within the parish itself. If we all think we are isolated, atomistic, persons who are "free" to pursue what each wants, then this attitude does little to foster the courage needed to abide by costly moral decisions. Our spiritual heritage holds that one can only abide by costly moral decisions if he or she draws strength from beyond the self. Hence, for the believer, there is a necessity to link moral growth and the Good News of Christ. In the following example we see how Catholics imbued with evangelical truths may foster moral courage.

Several years ago, as a response to a course of study he took in his parish, a laborer named Steve quit his job at a nuclear weapons parts manufacturing plant. Over the course of his study, for obvious reasons, Steve focused his attention on the documents of the Church regarding war and peace, particularly *The Challenge of Peace* and *Gaudium et Spes*.[53] He became fascinated with the Church's strong presumption against violence and war, and eventually was moved to make a decision in conscience to quit his job at the weapons parts plant.

Through his participation in the adult education program, he established a close relationship with his pastor and some other members of the parish. Upon hearing about Steve's action the pastor sought the help of the parish to assist with any of Steve's needs. As the pastor saw it, the parish had a duty to help Steve, because his act of quitting his job was a form of preaching the Gospel. Most persuasive to the parish small group was the fact that Steve came to his decision to leave his work at the plant based upon his study of explicitly Catholic sources of moral wisdom. The group rallied around Steve and set up a network of parishioners to help him find a job and assist with any temporary financial needs. In time, Steve did find other labor.

---

[53] U.S. Bishops, "The Challenge of Peace: God's Promise and Our Response," Pastoral Letter on War and Peace, *Origins* 13 (May 19, 1983): 1-32. See also *Gaudium et Spes* 77ff.

One could argue that it was not the moral *duty* of the parish to assist Steve, but simply an occasion for the parish to practice charity toward one of their members. The key ingredient in this story, however, is that Steve discerned his moral choice *within* the parish community, using *Catholic* sources of conscience formation. One wonders if more Catholics would abide by the teachings of the Church if they knew the parish community would stand behind them in solidarity.[54] Now, of course, the teaching of the Church does not tell people to quit their jobs if employed by nuclear weapons manufacturers. That decision was a prudential judgment by Steve and not a universal moral duty. Steve's actions are illustrative of where conscience and prudence might take us if we are formed by and live in such a supportive parish. But who is explicitly forming parish membership in the needed virtue of courage?

As the *Catechism* teaches, the law and doctrine of the faith is a light to conscience.[55] The parish can be a gathering place of persons who seek this light, and then seek further to have what is shown to them within this light clarified by and directed to the good. Thus, the parish can become a living source of tradition and a living discernment center based on prudence imbued with faith, hope, and love. To aspire to become this fascinating center of discernment, all the people, on a practical level, ought to be *informed* of this dignified mission and *formed* in two basic virtues: listening for and to the truth, and prudently carrying it out. Further, pastoral leaders ought to explicitly seek out these virtues in their own lives, so that they can be competent guides in people's moral and spiritual conversion. These virtues will be further explored in Chapter Three.

---

[54] *Catechism* 900, 1942.
[55] *Catechism* 1962, 1971.

III. CONCLUSION

We can see this current moment in the Catholic parish as a time of purification, a time of distinguishing what is of our faith and what is simply of culture and devoid of Christian life. It is not that the culture is graceless, but it has simply made itself less available to grace in its quest for independence from ecclesial and biblical authority.

As with all conversion, we start with an awareness of turning from sin and toward the Good, or more personally, to God. The source of true judgments of conscience is a heart converted to the Lord.[56] Pivotal to any parish moral renewal is this idea that there is a spiritual foundation to judgments of conscience. In this view, morality (which becomes a facet of spirituality), evangelization and even re-evangelization can be placed in a properly pastoral context.

This conversion process has to take on flesh within the circumstances of the parish. It does not have to take the form of another program. Rather it might be creatively integrated throughout existing structures. But we believe that for God to move us from our current state of unrest over moral questions, the renewal must be explicit, intentional, and flow from the prayer of the pastor and the people. As Catholics, where do people go to work out moral problems if not the parish?

> Lacking institutions for open dialogue on life problems we are prone to stumble from crisis to crisis, internalizing our failures — in the ensuing personal weakness, security is sought in media-dictated symbols of the good life.[57]

The heart has to be prepared for the God of the living. It is the parish, not the media, which should do this preparation. Ethics is

---

[56] *Veritatis Splendor* 64.

[57] Gary L. Sapp, ed. *Handbook of Moral Development: Models, Processes, Techniques and Research* (Birmingham, AL: Religion Education Press, 1986) 179.

about living, and it needs a corresponding experience of the living God to anchor its efforts to grow in virtue and hope. Without this mystical anchor, people will give up and find security in the cultural values, which can be devoid of the Christian power to renew. The *Catechism* calls prayer the life of the new heart.[58] And the new heart is formed in the parish community.

As Catholics, we have a tradition, we have what the secular world is thirsting for: roots. Theologians have given us the theory; the values of democratic capitalism (among other cultural sources) have given us an emphasis on experience; and now the *Catechism*, *Veritatis Splendor*, and *Evangelium Vitae* have given us a current articulation of a religious moral tradition. In light of our current cultural state and with the appearance of these ecclesial documents, it is appropriate to say that the parish is ripe for moral renewal. It is time for a family reunion. It is time to rediscover our roots, our identity, what really distinguishes us and gives us life. One thing Catholics have done well since the end of World War II in the U.S. is blend in, become American. Now is the time for us to reappropriate what it means to live as *Catholic* as well. This living is not a response in fear, but a response out of loving attention to God's voice in consciences formed in the midst of the parish. The *Catechism*'s gift to us will reside in how well the occasion of its appearance was grasped as an ecclesial invitation for all to once again love the good in God.

---

[58] *Catechism* 2697.

Chapter Two

THE LITURGY AND THE VISION
OF THE MORAL LIFE

I. INTRODUCTION

The liturgy is at the center of parish life. It is the clearest barometer of the health and vision of a parish community. It is in the liturgy that the parish gathers and expresses who it is and how it tries to live out its values. It is for this reason that the lack of participation in the liturgy is truly deadly for the life of the community. It is in the gathering together of the members of the community that the Gospel vision is articulated and made relevant to our ordinary lives. It is in the assembly of the faithful that people are given the strength and enthusiasm to continue for another week.

Sometimes people want to go to church to get some comfort. There is nothing wrong in that and hopefully that does happen. It would be a tragedy, however, if that were all that happened. People should also be challenged when they come to celebrate the Eucharist. If the Gospel message is preached it is one that is countercultural. The message of life, peace, and justice is loud and clear in the Gospel. This message should never be watered down so as not to disturb the community. Some people used to say half-jokingly, "May the peace of Christ disturb you."

Beginning the liturgy with the penitential rite reflects a spe-

33

cific understanding of human nature. There was wisdom in structuring the liturgy in this way. When we gather on Sunday and reflect over the past week, we need to take stock as to how well we attempted to implement the Gospel vision in our environment. The liturgy is about conversion to the vision of the Gospel and the teaching of the Church. We often resist the radical implications of what this means. The liturgy is the ongoing reminder.

II. COMMUNITY: THE NEW PARADIGM

Over the centuries the liturgy has been understood and expressed in a variety of ways. A debate on how we celebrate the liturgy took place at the Second Vatican Council. The debate still continues some thirty years later. The conversation is an important one because what we do in the liturgy symbolizes the whole of the Christian vision.

The reformed liturgy of the Council rests on the paradigm of community. The liturgy calls forth a community that interacts by singing, sharing ministries, offering the sign of peace, and acknowledging God in one another. The reformed liturgy does not invite one into a private and isolated worship. If the liturgy is private and compartmentalized then so is religion and the moral life. The reformed liturgy challenges the faith community to get involved in preparing the liturgy. It is not magic. It is not a matter of just going to church to get grace on Sunday. The one who presides at the liturgy calls the assembly to prayer by focusing its attention on each member's relationship to God and with one another. He invites the community to participate fully in the liturgical action. He challenges the people to carry the message of the liturgy into the world in word and deed.

A key insight of the liturgical renewal of the Second Vatican Council is the theology of the paschal mystery. The liturgy is a memorial of Christ's dying and rising. Along with Christ we are called to empty ourselves in order to experience the power of the resurrection. Christians who participate in the liturgy cannot escape this call from within the realities of everyday life. It is only there that the paschal mystery can be experienced. Christ had the ability to embrace and accept the Father's call to fidelity, which enabled him to speak the ultimate "Yes" from the cross. It is our imitation of Christ in saying our "Yeses" that lead us to the core of living out the Christian moral vision.

Pope Pius XII, in his encyclical on the liturgy, *Mediator Dei*, wrote that the liturgy is the continued exercise of the priestly office of Christ, "the public worship which our Redeemer offers to the heavenly Father and which the community of Christ's faithful pays to its Founder, and through him to the eternal Father; briefly, it is the whole public worship of the Mystical Body of Jesus Christ, Head and members."[1] Clearly the liturgy is not only a cultic ritual. It is an event that calls us to do in the world what Christ did in the world. The Second Vatican Council continued in this line of thought when the Council Fathers wrote that "the liturgy is the summit toward which the activity of the Church is directed; at the same time it is the fountain from which all power flows."[2]

To put it in another way, the purpose of the liturgy is to celebrate the mysterious presence of God among us in the community of believers. In this encounter we praise and adore God and are in return loved and challenged by God. We can even go so far as to say that all of our assumptions and behaviors are measured by the yardstick of worship. The liturgy and its message directly challenge the status quo to conform itself to the values and ideals of the Gospel.

The liturgical process is one of deification. By this we mean humanity's sharing in the life of God. Indeed the whole cosmos in some way shares in this divine life in that all things are created and sustained in God. The centrality of Christ as the beginning and

---

[1] Denzinger-Schönmetzer 3841, see J. Neuner, S.J. and J. Dupuis, S.J., *The Christian Faith* (New York: Alba House, 1996) 484, #1218; also *New Dictionary of Catholic Spirituality* 604.

[2] "The Constitution on the Sacred Liturgy," *Vatican Council II*, ed. Austin Flannery (Grand Rapids, MI: Costello Publishing Co., 1987), art. 10, p. 6.

end of creation is at the heart of this process of deification. This is exactly what we mean when we conclude the Eucharistic Prayer with the doxology, "Through Him, with Him, in Him, in the unity of the Holy Spirit, all glory and honor is yours, Almighty Father, forever and ever."

Through Christ the whole universe is to be transformed into God's likeness. When the community celebrates the liturgy it declares its willingness to be converted and to be instruments in bringing about the conversion of the world. It is for this reason that the liturgy invites a dynamic involvement of the community. Liturgy is not something to be watched. Each liturgy is different because the community and its emotional, spiritual, social, and political needs change each time they gather. Every word and every minute of the liturgy calls for our full attention and transformation. At its very essence the liturgy is about growth in the values of the kingdom and in the life of virtue that makes the kingdom visible. The liturgy calls the community into virtue, gives it the strength needed to become virtuous, and the power to live the songs we sing and the prayers we pray.

III. WHAT WE PRAY IS WHAT WE BELIEVE

The ancient axiom, "*lex orandi, lex credendi*" — the "law of praying is the law of believing" — asserts that all of our beliefs are in some way contained in our prayers. Prayer not only expresses what is in the heart but also articulates what is in the mind. For example, we begin and end every prayer, "In the name of the Father, and of the Son, and of the Holy Spirit." Only Christians can pray in this way because Jesus revealed a God who is Triune. Early councils of the Church struggled with the question of the identity of Jesus and his articulation of the trinitarian God, praying, "In the name of the Father, and of the Son, and of the Holy Spirit." It reflects a very basic Christian belief that is numbered among the dogmas of the Church.

Since the Eucharist is the Christian prayer *par excellence* there is no better place to look for a summary of the Christian life than in the theological underpinnings of the Eucharistic Prayers. The Eucharist is the center of the Christian life for it is in this liturgical context that the community proclaims and celebrates the life, death, and resurrection of Jesus Christ. Every dimension of the Christian life is in some way summarized and expressed in the Eucharist. This certainly includes the values and virtues inherent in the Christian moral life. Christians participate in the life of God through Jesus Christ. The centrality of the Eucharist is the community's clearest expression of its relationship to Christ and its commitment to the moral principles of the Gospel.

The Eucharistic Prayers are rich in their expression of the essential values of the Christian life. In the First Eucharistic Prayer we pray, "Grant us your peace in this life, save us from final damnation, and count us among those you have chosen."[3] The word for peace in Hebrew is "Shalom." Shalom suggests that what was broken is now fixed. The word implies that there is a basic flaw in human nature that is patched or repaired by God. This most clearly happens in the covenant that God makes with his people. The covenant or relationship that we have with God brings about shalom; it makes whole that which was broken through human sinfulness. The underlying assumption in this prayer statement is that God does not wish our damnation (cf. Jn 3:17). Instead God wishes us shalom so that we might be fully free to share in God's life. The priestly prayer of Jesus in John's Gospel (17:1-26) reflects Jesus' wish of shalom for those who follow him. In that prayer it is evident that this shalom comes from sharing in the very relationship that Jesus has with God.

We pray in the Second Eucharistic Prayer, "We thank you for counting us worthy to stand in your presence and serve you."[4]

---

[3] *The Roman Missal: The Sacramentary* (New York: Catholic Book Publishing Co., 1985) 544.

[4] *Roman Missal* 550.

The two verbs used here, "stand" and "serve" assume relationships. We can stand with God to the degree that we live justly. We can stand with God because through right behavior we reflect God more vibrantly to the world. It is the process of conversion that makes the likeness of God more and more evident in believers. The underlying belief expressed in this prayer is that we have been made in God's image but have often distorted this reflection of God's image through our choice of sin. The whole goal of the moral life is the renewing and restoring of that likeness through behaviors and actions that are in harmony with the community's beliefs and teachings. Service is the fundamental behavior of one who is conformed to God's image and likeness. To serve implies a desire to please and do what is good for another. Through our service of God and neighbor, we declare that we desire to please God and others through the gift of love. This is the fundamental choice that every Christian must make. The barometer of the quality of our moral lives is the way we live out that choice of serving through our gift of love.

We pray in the Third Eucharistic Prayer, "From age to age, you gather a people to yourself.... Grant that we who are nourished by his body and blood, may be filled with his Holy Spirit, and become one body, one spirit in Christ."[5] It is the Spirit of God who moves us to embrace the virtues of the moral life. St. Paul says it well in his letter to the Galatians,

> Walk according to the Spirit, and don't carry out the desires of the flesh.... Now it is evident what the works of the flesh are — fornication, impurity and indecent acts, idolatry, sorcery, hatred, strife, jealousy, outbursts of anger, selfishness, envy, dissension, factionalism, drunkenness, carousing, and the like. I warn you now as I warned you before, that those who do such things will not inherit the Kingdom of God. In contrast the

---

[5] *Roman Missal* 552.

> fruit of the Spirit is love, joy, peace, patience, kindness,
> goodness, faith, gentleness, and self-control.... If we live
> in the Spirit, let us also follow the Spirit (Gal 5:16-25).

The Christian life is a day-to-day attentiveness to the voice of the Holy Spirit. To the extent that we listen to the Spirit is there harmony and integrity in our lives. It is through the Spirit that we become single-minded in our vision of life and in living in this way we become one body, one Spirit in Christ.

We pray in the Fourth Eucharistic Prayer, "You formed us in your own likeness.... Even when we disobeyed you and lost your friendship, you did not abandon us to the power of death, but helped us all to seek and find you.... Grant also to us, your children, to enter into our heavenly inheritance."[6] This prayer celebrates the history of salvation. God never abandons fallen humanity but constantly calls us anew to become what God has created us to be. All of the Christian life is about seeking the One who is the ultimate source of our happiness. St. Augustine articulated this so well when he wrote, "Our hearts, O God, are restless until they rest in Thee."[7]

The Fourth Eucharistic Prayer is especially profound in its vision of the moral life. The purpose of human life to guard and protect all of creation is expressed in the beginning of the prayer. Even though humankind constantly fails in its mission, God keeps on calling us to conversion. The prayer acknowledges our tendency to be selfish. "That we might live, no longer for ourselves," the Spirit is sent to pull us out of our self-concern and to move us to live in correct relationships with others. Every time we pray this prayer we are reminded of one of the essential components of the moral life: self-giving.

In the First Eucharistic Prayer for reconciliation we pray, "From the beginning of time you have always done what is good

---

6 *Roman Missal* 557.
7 St. Augustine, *The Confessions of St. Augustine*, ed. John E. Rotelle, O.S.A. (NY: New City Press, 1995), Book 1, p. 39.

for us so that we might be holy as you are holy."[8] The vocation of the Christian is to become a saint. This goal is expressed in some way in all of the Eucharistic Prayers. It is most eloquently expressed in the Eucharistic Preface for Holy Men and Holy Women I:

> Father, all powerful and ever living God… you are glorified in your saints, for their glory is the crowning of your gifts. In their lives on earth, you give us an example. In our communion with them, you give us their friendship. In their prayer for the Church, you give us strength and protection. This great company of witnesses spurs us on to victory, to share their prize of everlasting glory, through Jesus Christ our Lord.[9]

A similar sentiment is expressed in the Eucharistic Preface for Holy Men and Women II:

> You renew the Church in every age by raising up men and women outstanding in holiness, living witnesses of your unchanging love. They inspire us by their heroic lives, and help us by their constant prayers to be the living sign of your saving power.[10]

We are fortunate in our tradition to have so many outstanding men and women who serve as examples for us in living the moral life. They show us the way and prove that it is possible to do what is right and good. Page after page of the Sacramentary praises the many marvelous disciples of Jesus over the past two thousand years. It is critical that we always recall their example so that we might respond to the same call to holiness in our day. Lawrence Cunningham puts it well, "The life of the saint should

---

[8] *Roman Missal* 1123.
[9] *Roman Missal* 511.
[10] *Roman Missal* 513.

act as a parable. It should shock us into a heightened and new sense of God's presence and judgment in our own lives."[11]

The genius of the saints' accomplishments is really summarized in the Second Eucharistic Prayer for Reconciliation, "You gave him up to death so that we might turn again to you and find our way to one another."[12] The saints were men and women who focused on Christ and thus daily tried to find a way to be present to God and to the people who came into their lives. Pope John Paul II reiterated the sentiments expressed in this particular Eucharistic Prayer:

> Therefore, if we wish to keep in mind this community of the people of God, which is so vast and so extremely differentiated, we must see first and foremost Christ saying in a way to each member of the Community: "Follow me." It is the community of disciples, each of whom in a different way — at times very consciously and consistently, at other times not very consciously and very consistently — is following Christ. This shows us the deeply "personal" aspect and dimension of this society.[13]

The Eucharist is about communion with God and one another. This community that forms around the table is indeed a community of disciples. The saints were people who not only looked at Christ but also patterned their lives after his. There is no clearer place where we model for the world who we are as a community of disciples than around the Eucharistic table. In our gathering there is a message that we are a community of saints and sinners striving to live according to the values and principles that Jesus taught by word and example.

---

[11] Lawrence Cunningham, *The Meaning of Saints* (San Francisco: Harper and Row, 1980) 79.

[12] *Roman Missal* 1129.

[13] Pope John Paul II, *Redemptor Hominis* (Redeemer of Humankind), March 4, 1979 (Washington, DC: United States Catholic Conference, 1979) 21.

IV. THE PASCHAL MYSTERY: THE RHYTHM OF
THE CHRISTIAN LIFE

We have stated throughout these chapters that the Christian life is an ongoing process. It is never a once-and-for-all event. The process takes place in the choices we make every day. Oftentimes people expect that Christian behavior should always reflect what Christians say. Sometimes people expect Christians to be a finished product. It is like the story of the group of students standing outside an Over-Eaters Anonymous clinic. These students stood and watched the clients coming out. Their reaction was, "Look at them. What hypocrites! They're all still fat."

In Baptism, *being* a Christian happens in an instant. *Becoming* a Christian takes a lifetime. The theological phrase that expresses this lifetime process is called *the paschal mystery.* This phrase simply means that through their baptism Christians enter into this lifetime process of becoming like Christ by incorporating their life experiences into the dying and rising of the Lord Jesus.

The paradigm of the paschal mystery was popularized by the German Benedictine monk, Dom Odo Casel, who died in 1948. The Second Vatican Council adapted this image in several of its documents, most notably in *Sacrosanctum Concilium,* the Constitution on the Sacred Liturgy. One of the great achievements of the Second Vatican Council was to underscore the importance of the concept of the paschal mystery. Since all Christian prayer either leads to the Eucharist or flows from it, in some way it is an experience of the dying and rising of the Lord Jesus.

What is especially significant about the revival of the concept of the paschal mystery is that it incorporates the entire Christ-event, i.e., his birth, life, death, resurrection, and ascension. These events cannot be separated into different categories. It is the entire Christ-event that brings about salvation. The word "paschal" embodies this reality. The use of this word helps us avoid focusing only on the cross or only on the resurrection. Both realities are equally included in the word "paschal."

This word "paschal" comes from the Hebrew, "Pesach," and

refers to the Passover, Israel's deliverance from the Egyptians when the angel of death passed over the door posts marked by the lamb's blood. The form of this annual remembrance of Passover was influenced by the spring rituals of the surrounding cultures. For the Jews, however, it was much more than a celebration of the freshness of springtime. It was a festival of redemption. At the annual Passover meal, the Jews remembered their deliverance from slavery to the Egyptians. In doing so they were not only remembering a past event, but also celebrating that Yahweh was still with them and would walk with them into the future. Each Jew was challenged to internalize this event into his or her own life. In other words, the gift of freedom was given to the Jewish people collectively but each Jew was given that gift in his or her personal life experience.

It was precisely in the context of the Passover meal that Jesus promised his body and blood for the salvation of the world. He is the new paschal lamb and it is through his blood that we are freed from the slavery of sin. The author of the letter to the Hebrews captured these thoughts when he wrote:

> But when Christ came as the high priest of the good things that have come to be, he passed through that greater and more perfect tabernacle not made by human hands, that is, not belonging to this creation, and entered once and for all into the sanctuary, not with the blood of goats and calves but with his own blood, thus obtaining eternal redemption for us. For if the sprinkling of blood from rams and bulls and the ashes of a heifer can sanctify those who are ritually unclean so that their flesh is purified, how much more will the blood of Christ, who through the eternal Spirit offered himself unblemished to God, cleanse our consciences from dead works to worship the living God (Heb 9:11-14).

It is in the worship of the living God that the Christian continues the work of redemption. What does this mean? It means to do what

Christ did, that is, to empty and sacrifice oneself so that life may come to others.

Wisdom for the Christian means patterning one's life on Christ's life. The baptized Christian is called to mirror in his or her life what Christ did in his life. Such a conformity to Christ underlies the meaning of the word "mystery" in the liturgical context. Mystery means that it is not totally comprehensible or even visible how each Christian continues the process of Christ's dying and rising in the patterns of his/her daily life. This conformity or becoming like Christ is a mystery because we cannot program how this will happen for each Christian. There is more that is unknown and unseen in the subtleties of living out the Christian life in the midst of the world. It is essential to understand that a "paschal mystery" spirituality has more to do with taking on Christ's attitude than simply mimicking his actions. St. Paul in his letter to the Philippians expressed it well:

> Have the same attitude among yourselves that Christ Jesus had, who, though he was in the form of God, did not consider equality with God something to hold on to. Instead, he emptied himself and took on the form of a slave, being born in human likeness, and to all appearances a man. He humbled himself and became obedient, even unto death, death on a cross. Because of this, God greatly exalted him and bestowed on him the name that is above every other name, so that at the name of Jesus every knee shall bend, in the heavens, on earth, and below the earth. And every tongue will proclaim to the glory of God the Father that Jesus Christ is Lord (Ph 2:5-11).

Each Christian then is invited to take on the attitude that Christ had towards life. The Holy Spirit moves individual Christians to do this in particular ways that will vary from person to person. Christians who take their call seriously must listen carefully in prayer for how to pattern their lives on that of Christ.

Mother Teresa, for example, did this in a way that was faithful to the promptings of the Spirit as she heard them. Archbishop Romero lived out the paschal mystery in another way that was faithful to his perception of the call of the Spirit. The living out of the paschal mystery will be different for each individual.

The paschal mystery in our lives has much to do with a rediscovery in our time of the humanity of Christ. When the Council of Chalcedon defined that Christ was fully human and fully divine, most people believed the divine aspect of Christ's personality but often paid lip service to his humanity. In 1950, some fifteen hundred years later, the question of the relationship of Christ's humanity to his divinity was reintroduced once again. Contemporary theologians have gained a new appreciation of the "fully human" aspect of Christ's personality. The Second Vatican Council endorsed this renewed understanding in its statement that Christ "worked with human hands. He thought with a human mind. He acted with a human will and he loved with a human heart. Born of the Virgin Mary, he has truly been made one of us, like to us in all things but sin."[14]

The implications of this for living out the paschal mystery are very important. The fact that Christ was really human means that he lived out his human existence exactly as we do and was not just play-acting. He lived out the paschal mystery in the everyday ordinariness of his human existence, as well as in his sacrifice on the cross. We, too, live out the paschal mystery in the midst of the messiness of everyday life, and in the arena of the marketplace. This makes the liturgy challenging. We are not just recalling a past event. We are re-enacting it in the here and now with our eyes fixed on the future. "*Ite, Missa Est,*" "Go, the Mass is ended," are among the most important words spoken at the liturgy. These are the words that send Christians forth into the world to live the Eucharist, to become like Christ in his dying and rising in the midst of

---

[14] "The Church in the Modern World," in *Vatican Council II*, ed. Austin Flannery (Grand Rapids, MI: Costello Publishing Co., 1978), art. 22, p. 903.

their everyday lives. In faithfully dying to self and rising to a fidelity to God, the Catholic becomes a powerful moral force in society.

V. THE LITURGY AND CONVERSION

Each time we celebrate the liturgy we are challenged to change. We are confronted with the way we live life every time we come to the Eucharist. If one sincerely participates in the liturgy, it is impossible not to experience the liturgy as a mirror that is held up before our lives. We are challenged to do better and to bring our lives more in conformity with the values of the Gospel.

Conversion or change is a difficult topic to comprehend. Bernard Lonergan wrote that there are three types of conversion. The first is *intellectual conversion.* Our intellectual constructs and concepts often need to be renewed. It is hard to let go of the way we put our worlds together. But the force of truth softens our hardened thought patterns and frees us to "think again." In welcoming truth, we are ready for *moral conversion.* This means that we have changed to welcome what is truly of value for us as mature human beings. It is not enough to claim that we think differently or that we have seen the light. Our behaviors must manifest the new insights we have. The final and highest form of conversion is *religious conversion.* By this, Lonergan means that we fall in love with God.[15] It is the falling in love with God that will ground the Christian in ethical behavior that flows out of a deep faith in the divine. When we are really in love, we want to act in a way that will please and serve the beloved.

The theme of conversion is a consistent one in the Hebrew Scriptures. The prophets constantly called Israel back to the covenant. The stubbornness that is so much a part of human nature is borne out in Israel's history of wandering away from the cov-

---

[15] Bernard Lonergan, *Method in Theology* (New York: Seabury Press, 1972). In this important volume Lonergan presents a methodology for studying theology that includes conversation with the other disciplines.

enant. A monk recently picked up on the universality of this tendency. Some people asked him, "Brother, what do you do all day long?" His first impulse was to review his daily schedule with them. But he had a second thought. "What do I really do all day long?" He thought about it for a few moments and responded, "This is what I do all day long. I fall down and keep on getting back up again." The prophets were persistent in their invitation to Israel to get back up again.

The same idea is carried through the Christian Scriptures. John the Baptist preached a message of repentance and renewal and Jesus called for a complete conversion and reorientation of the human heart. The reorientation that both preached was radical. It required that ones' affections, goals, and actions be continuously purified. The essential challenge is that it is not only a falling in love with God, but a staying in love and growing in love. That is the work of a lifetime.

The liturgy is an ongoing reminder of this call to conversion. For this reason it is essential that we bring a spirit of humility to the liturgy. The word "humility" comes from the Latin "humus," meaning earth. The one who is humble is close to the earth. People who are humble have their feet firmly planted on the ground. St. Bonaventure wrote, "What a person is before God that he is and nothing more."[16] The one who is humble recognizes that all comes from God and that we can do nothing without God's help.

Once we recognize this reality, we must admit our weaknesses and ask for the assistance that we need from God and the community during the liturgy. This can be a frightening prospect because it requires much trust. The principles of Alcoholics Anonymous capture this dynamic quite well. After we acknowledge our mistakes, AA teaches that we must rely on a "Higher Power." This is solid teaching. The goals of the Christian moral life are really beyond human grasp. It is not sufficient to rely on our efforts alone.

---

[16] St. Bonaventure, *The Soul's Journey Into God,* in *Bonaventure,* tr. Ewert Cousins (New York: Paulist Press, 1978). In this classic work, St. Bonaventure gives his theology of the spiritual journey and his view of the human person who makes this journey.

We need God's help to live this way. Our faith teaches us that the same Spirit that calls us to conversion guides us all along the way. We must trust that what is impossible for us is possible for God. To live a converted Christian life, one of deep faith and moral consistency, can only be done with God's grace.

A poignant symbol for conversion based on humility and trust is the Gospel story of the washing of the feet (Jn 13). In the Johannine communities, the washing of feet was considered as a sacrament on a par with the Eucharist. The whole experience was essentially Eucharistic: Jesus on his knees, humble before God and his disciples, washes feet. His powerful message is that if he who is our Lord and Master can do this then so must we. This is the goal of the Christian life. If conversion is real, it must manifest itself in our service of neighbor. It is not enough to confess sin. If we are really open to grace and if our affections are truly transformed, we will begin to live differently. The moral life is not an abstraction. It is concrete living. The English Benedictine, Dom Chapman, articulated it well when he wrote, "If you need to know how you are doing, then look to the charity of your life."[17] The liturgy is the place where we meet God and the community of believers. It is here that our life of love of God and neighbor is examined and celebrated each week. St. Basil once wrote that if we did not have one another then we would not have feet to wash. If we *live our liturgy*, it leads to foot washing: to the respect and service of all human life. The moral life of the Church is nothing other than an expression of that respect.

VI. THE LITURGY AND LISTENING

The saints were women and men who placed a high priority on the liturgy and were formed by the lessons learned there, espe-

---

[17] Sr. Ellen Joyce, "Pray as You Can: The Theory of Prayer of John Chapman," diss., Fordham University, 1981. Chapter Three (pp. 97-143) is an excellent explanation of John Chapman's theology of prayer.

cially in the reading of the Scriptures. To give one example from many, St. Francis of Assisi was at the Eucharist when he heard the Gospel proclaimed about the rich young man. He was so moved by the story that it caused him to take a second look at how he was living his life. This particular reading within the liturgy had a special power and impact on him. In fact, the story of the rich young man became the source of St. Francis' moral and religious imagination.

The Gospels tell us only a few things about what it means to be a disciple of Jesus Christ. These few things, however, have the power to radically impact the lives of those who choose to live the Christian life. To be a disciple of Jesus is to give up everything, take up the cross, and to walk in the footsteps of the Lord (see Mk 1:16-20). As we have seen, disciples usually fluctuate in the consistency of their response, but God remains forever faithful.

God is relentless in the challenge he extends to us to grow morally. The liturgy is the place where this call regularly happens week by week year after year. The text of the liturgy and the Scriptures are prayed in a different context each week because we change from week to week. We are invited to look at our culture, how we are influenced by it, and how we are called to transform it. Through the power of the Eucharist, the gathered community becomes supportive of its members who are attempting to become the body of Christ in the midst of the world.

Jesus taught his disciples to pray, and he also taught them how to be a community (Lk 11:1-4; Lk 10:1). This is what parishes should be about, i.e., praying communities reaching out to one another and to the world as a force for the moral good. The community through its prayer and interaction has a collective wisdom. All who gather for its liturgy must listen with ears, mind, and heart to the wisdom of the community. This wisdom is different from mere learning. Wisdom comes from an attentive listening and always calls for concrete actions and behaviors. The task of seeking the wisdom of the Christian moral life is a lifetime endeavor.

Jesus modeled this for us in his teachings and actions. If we were to summarize in one sentence how Christ became a wise person, it would read like this: "Christ is the one who listened to the Father." Christ modeled wisdom by attentive listening. The challenge for us Christians living in the fast-paced culture of the United States is to learn how to slow down long enough to listen. The busyness of our lives makes listening difficult but not impossible. It is indeed a challenge to listen during the liturgy.

The kind of listening that we speak of here is what the prophet Elijah struggled with centuries ago. His story is a lesson for us today:

> Then the Lord said, "Go outside and stand on the mountain before the Lord; the Lord will be passing by." A strong and heavy wind was rending the mountains and crushing rocks before the Lord; but the Lord was not in the wind. After the wind there was an earthquake; but the Lord was not in the earthquake. After the earthquake, there was a fire; but the Lord was not in the fire. After the fire there was a tiny whispering sound. When he heard this, Elijah wrapped his face in his mantle and went out and stood at the entrance of the cave (1 K 19:11-13).

Today's Christian needs to learn to listen to these tiny whispering sounds. The noise of our culture so often drowns out the voice of truth. We need to re-acclimate ourselves to the whisperings of the Spirit.

Within the liturgy and within life in general, there are three voices that we need to tune ourselves into: the voices of self, others, and God. All three are important and all three are essential ingredients that form the wisdom of the community.

It can be said of listening what is often said of charity: it must begin at home. If we have not first learned to listen to our inner voices, it is naive to think even for a moment that we can hear God's voice. If we are not in touch with ourselves, how can we expect to be in touch with God and others? We live in a culture that does not foster a reflective attitude within us. Because many people are not reflective they do not live authentic moral lives and frequently make the same mistakes over and over again.

St. Ignatius of Loyola is the classic example within the Catholic tradition of reflective listening. For him, listening actually became the way to holiness. He learned to pay attention to the voices that were active within him. His acclaimed method for discerning the spirits came from this simple listening to self. He noticed the differences between those things that brought him lasting inner peace from those voices that gave momentary pleasure but no lasting peace. This kind of listening gave St. Ignatius a clear indication of the kinds of choices that he should make.

He acquired this kind of self-knowledge through a lot of effort. It required uncompromising honesty to face himself as he truly was. From him we learn that taking the mask off, being oneself before God, is the beginning of wisdom. In attempting to communicate this wisdom to us, St. Ignatius suggests the "examination of consciousness." This way is deeper and more biblically rooted than what we commonly mean by "examination of conscience." Rather than taking a minimalist approach of examining the things we have done or not done, the greater challenge is to examine our consciousness. What is going on inside of us? What are our needs, fears, angers, hurts, and loves? If we don't ask these kinds of questions, we will miss the deeper realities of life and the movements of God's Spirit within us.

If we can listen to the tiny whispering sounds within us, then we will more likely be attentive to listening to God and others within the liturgy in our parish community. In this communal setting, we are challenged to move beyond ourselves to learn from the collective wisdom of our Catholic heritage. For Christians, wisdom is incomplete if it does not include the teachings of the Church and its long moral tradition. If we truly listen during the liturgy, we can be inspired by the words and actions of men and women who have walked before us during the past two thousand years.

In Chapter Three we will reflect further on how discernment

takes place for individuals and the community. The cultivation of wisdom is the key for developing the Christian virtues and moral living. It is critical to accept the premise that wisdom blossoms in a living community that treasures wisdom and the virtuous living that flows from it.

VII. PRAYING AND THE MORAL LIFE

As we have seen, all prayer, and especially liturgical prayer, challenges us to live with moral integrity. There is something beautiful about the warmth of God's presence that we can come to know in prayer. There is also something very demanding about how we are to live life once we have been touched by God.

The new *Catechism of the Catholic Church* has some beautiful things to teach about the meaning of prayer and the living out of the moral life. The last chapter of the *Catechism* entitled "Christian Prayer" is especially moving. Prayer is described as a covenant relationship, a communion of hearts with God and all human beings. The authors note that the Hebrew Scriptures are a dialogue of prayer between God and the Jewish people. They describe the Psalms as the crescendo of this teaching which provide wonderful models for prayer. The spectrum of emotions in the Psalms capture so much of the exuberance and the struggle of human nature.

The *Catechism* goes on to teach that prayer finds its perfection in Jesus. Especially in Luke's Gospel, Jesus is portrayed as praying prior to all of the significant moments in his life. The prayer of Jesus continues in the community of the Church. The Acts of the Apostles is the early community's adventure into the "life of prayer" mode led by Jesus and inspired by the Spirit. As such, this community comes to experience the Eucharist as the centerpiece of its experience of prayer.

Reflecting on the experience of the disciples, it becomes clear that Jesus formed them in the way of prayer. It is noteworthy that Jesus first gives them a glimpse of his goodness. This was his way of whetting their appetites. This paradigm is especially evident in the account of his transfiguration:

> Now it happened that about eight days after he had said this, he took Peter, John, and James and went up the mountain to pray. While he was praying the appearance of his face was altered and his clothing became dazzlingly white. And behold, two men were conversing with him, Moses and Elijah, who were seen in glory and spoke of his exodus which he was to accomplish in Jerusalem. Peter and his companions had been overcome by sleep, but awakening fully, they saw his glory and the two men standing with him. As the men were about to leave him, Peter said to Jesus, "Master, it is good that we are here; let us make three tents, one for you, one for Moses, and one for Elijah," not really knowing what he was saying. While he was speaking, a cloud came and overshadowed them, and they became frightened when they entered the cloud. Then out of the cloud came a voice that said, "This is my Son, my Chosen One; listen to him." After the voice had spoken, Jesus was found alone. They fell silent and told no one in those days anything they had seen (Lk 9:28-36).

The transfiguration was truly a liturgical experience. For Peter, James, and John it was a symbol of God's presence and power. When they glimpsed this reality, they changed significantly. This transformation signaled a fuller and more meaningful change that God would bring about at the end of time. The experience of the transfiguration was followed by the second prediction of the passion. The apostles were called to pattern their lives on Christ's life. This would necessarily entail practical, concrete expressions in their everyday lives. The apostles were invited to leave the comfort of Mount Tabor and begin the journey to Jerusalem. The cycle of prayer presented here is one that begins with an experience of God that then prepares one for the reality of the cross in the midst of everyday life. One must go down the mountain and get back to the routine of daily life. The way people live once they come down from the mountain and begin the journey to Jerusalem is the test of their faith and the strength of their relationship with the Lord. It is in this context that we can talk about the moral life, its principles and practicalities.

When we pray, it is the Spirit who leads us back to the community of believers and its wisdom. It is only when we pray that we can get to the heart of our Christian treasury of knowledge, beliefs, and virtues. An old adage says, "When someone reads the law, their first instinct is to figure out how to get around it." We would be naive not to acknowledge that this is part of the human psyche. Teachers and parish staff members need to be aware that it is not enough to simply mandate rules and regulations. People need to be persuaded and invited into a relationship with the one who is "the way, the truth, and the life" (Jn 14:6). St. Augustine's "Love and do what you will" is an excellent articulation of this reality. There is no limit to what people who are in love with God will do. To live by Christian values requires a strength that the dictates of the law in themselves cannot give. Bernard Lonergan once said that it is easy to be good when the people around us are being good. It is not so easy when they are not being good.[18] We live at a time when it is not easy to be good because of the secularistic values taught by our culture. More than ever, good moral living will depend on the depth of our relationship with God and the support that we give one another in the community.

Within the liturgy, the Lord's Prayer is the best example of the relationship between prayer and life. For this reason, the "Our Father" is the centerpiece of the *Catechism*'s teaching on prayer. Here we have a summary of the Gospel and the beautiful vision of

---

[18] Bernard Lonergan, *Insight: A Study of Human Understanding* (New York: Philosophical Library, 1957). Note especially Chapter XVIII, "The Possibility of Ethics," pp. 595-633.

the Christian way of life. Because of our baptism, we together call God "Our Father." This suggests a willingness to embrace the covenant that God offers to us. By imitating God in our lives we glorify God's name and invite others into that same reverence. We commit ourselves to be and do the things that will bring about the kingdom of God. The desire to do God's will is the acid test of the depth of our Christian commitment. Justice demands that we share the bread that we are given with the poor. Christians are called to the highest degree of forgiveness as taught by Christ and the witness of the martyrs, who conquered evil with good.[19] Ultimately, we need God's help to resist the temptations and evils that would make us settle for anything less than loving the Lord our God with our whole heart, soul, and strength, and our neighbor as ourselves (Mt 22:34-40). This is the heart of Christian morality and the message at the center of all prayer, especially liturgical prayer.

VIII. CONCLUSION

To paraphrase the *Constitution on the Sacred Liturgy*, the Eucharist is the source and summit of the moral life.[20] Christians are called to listen to the prophetic word and to give their assent to that word in the "Amen" of the Eucharist. That proclamation means that we have heard the word, measured our lives according to that word, and wish to receive the bread of life to strengthen us to live the message of that word. The Eucharist is the source of our unity for it is here that we assent to a common vision. It is here that the vision is spoken anew each day and renewed in every age.

The moral life of the Christian is one that extends beyond

---

[19] *Catechism of the Catholic Church* (Morristown, NJ: Silver Burdett Ginn, 1994) 681-683.

[20] *Sacrosanctum Concilium* (Constitution on the Sacred Liturgy). *Vatican Council II: The Conciliar and Post Conciliar Documents,* ed. Austin Flannery (Wilmington, DE: Scholarly Resources, 1975) 10.

our individual worlds. It immerses us into the larger world of our culture. It is not the culture that determines our manner of life in the world. It is the Gospel. Much of our prayer in the Eucharist is a reminder to us that the role of the Christian is to transform our culture through the Gospel values of peace and justice. Pope John Paul II expressed this goal in his encyclical, *Sollicitudo rei socialis*:

> Father, you have given all peoples one origin and your will for them is to gather them as one family in your-self. Fill the hearts of all men with the fire of your love and the desire to ensure justice for all their brothers and sisters. By sharing the good things you give us may we secure justice and equality for every human being, an end of all division, and a human society built on love and peace.[21]

The example of Jesus is one that teaches us how to live in peace and equality with all peoples. Those who choose to gather around the Eucharistic table give witness to that reality and promise to live according to these values.

The Preface for Eucharistic Prayer II for Reconciliation proclaims the goal of the Christian moral life and the means for attaining its ends:

> Father, all-powerful and ever-living God, we praise and thank you through Jesus Christ our Lord for your presence and action in the world. In the midst of conflict and division, we know it is you who turn our minds to thoughts of peace. Your Spirit changes our hearts; enemies begin to speak to one another, those who were estranged join hands in friendship, and nations seek the way of peace together. Your Spirit is at work when understanding puts an end to strife, when hatred is

---

[21] Pope John Paul II, *Sollicitudo rei socialis* (Boston, MA: St. Paul Books, 1987) 49.

quenched by mercy, and vengeance gives way to forgiveness. For this we should never cease to thank and praise you. We join with all the choirs of heaven as they sing forever to your glory.[22]

All that we are and all that we are destined to become is celebrated and renewed in every Eucharistic celebration. For this reason, the Eucharist is a living catechism for disciples. It teaches us to live in deeper communion with God and the world through a life of virtue and service.

---

[22] *Roman Missal* 1128.

CHAPTER THREE

THE PARISH COMMUNITY AND MORAL DISCERNMENT

I. INTRODUCTION

As we noted in Chapter One, the parish is the place where most Catholics experience the Church and the challenge of the Gospel life. The parish is the place where people should be invited into communion with God and friendship with one another. The challenge for pastoral staffs is to give concrete, practical ways for making all of this real for the people. After all the moral life is not primarily about abstractions. As Edward Collins Vacek writes:

> The first principle of Christian ethics is not "do good and avoid evil" but rather "love God" or "be with, be for, and cooperate with God." We begin with our experienced relation to God, not a relation to the good.[1]

All that we do in the parish is ultimately an invitation to be in relationship with God and others. From these relationships it becomes clearer as to what is morally good. The choices not to be

---

[1] Edward Collins Vacek, S.J., *Love, Human and Divine: The Heart of Christian Ethics* (Washington, DC: Georgetown University Press, 1994) 137.

good are always choices not to be in relationship. As we reflected in the previous chapter, all of the sacraments, but especially the Eucharist, are about relationships. The liturgy celebrates who we are as a people and what we are striving to become.

It is in this context that we will speak of discernment. Simply put, God's will is that we be in relationship with Him and with one another. Discernment is a process that helps people distinguish what choices assist us in being faithful to relationships with God and others. Given the fact that the parish is about relationships, it is one of the most logical places where the process of discernment can best occur.

II. THE PRIMARY AGENDA OF THE PARISH STAFF: FORM COMMUNITY

Christianity is essentially community. There is no Christianity without the Church community. For most Christians, the parish is the place where this is experienced. In an American culture built upon private initiative, it is indeed a challenge to build community. It is precisely because of our penchant for individualism that so many people today are longing for some kind of community. What kind of activities and dispositions assist us in forming community?

First and foremost, the pastor and staff should realize that they are symbols. On some level, they represent God for many people. They mediate God's love. It is not only their responsibility, but they are the key players. Specifically, the way parish staffs interact with people is important for conveying the message of God's love. It is hard to begin to appreciate God's friendship outside the context of human kindness, compassion, and gentleness. The actions of parish staff certainly speak louder than words.

Creating an atmosphere of friendship should be high on a parish staff's agenda. Fellowship after Sunday liturgies and warm, inviting gathering places in the Church, rectory and parish centers can help create this environment. In this kind of setting, people are given the opportunity to form friendships with one another that can powerfully mirror God's friendship.

Since we live in a society of broken friendships and relationships, the parish today has a special challenge to try to keep the vision of faithfulness in relationships alive and at the same time to be an instrument of healing. It is obvious that sacramental preparation and the celebrating of the various Rites of the Church offer countless opportunities for this. In addition, support groups for the bereaved, separated, and divorced can be powerful occasions of grace for those who hurt and doubt God's friendship and the possibility of human love.

The outreach to the poor and marginalized through committees that deal with social matters can offer special moments of encounter with God. Reaching out to these people and serving their needs is being concerned with what concerns God. For many, this is news. Even though there was always a social outreach in the Catholic vision prior to the Second Vatican Council, Catholic spirituality tended to be a very private affair. Usually serving others was seen as the fruit of one's prayer, not prayer itself. Since the Council there has been a heightened awareness of God's presence among the poor. We find God in them. The poor also become our teachers. They teach us how to pray. Their dependence on God and others is precisely the attitude of openness that is at the heart of all prayer.

It is important that we do not just send people forth to do nice things for others. In the parishes we should provide structured opportunities to reflect on our service to and with those in need. Theological refection is an opportunity for people to integrate their outreach to others within the total context of their spiritual life and moral vision. This can help to root people in a life of charity. They become, then, not simply "Do Gooders," but rather people formed by the Gospel. Through such reflection and sharing, people become more aware that the choices they make are important and affect their relationship with God and the world.[2]

Another important task for every parish staff in forming the community is attention to marriage preparation. We are painfully aware that so many couples who come for marriage preparation do not have a faith life. The first impulse for many of us is to emphasize the rules and to call people to task for breaking the rules. We need to resist that temptation. As we have noted, moral living is the fruit of a relationship with God. We need to invite people into that relationship. Most couples who come to the Church to be married do not have a conscious awareness of these realities. The pastoral agenda is to awaken this in them.[3] We will discuss marriage preparation further in the next chapter.

Finally, the greatest contribution the parish can make is to give people experiences of love that are truly biblically rooted. It is not necessary to belabor the point that many people in our society have very weak or shallow notions of what love is all about. We should be careful not to assume that people understand the biblical depth of such words as "friendship" and *caritas*. Edward Vacek points out,

> Most Christian authors praise a self-sacrificing love or a love that works for the other; some praise a love by which we live from others; unfortunately, only a few

---

[2] Parish staffs might wish to study methods of theological reflection. This kind of reflection should also go on among themselves. Theological reflection usually begins with a text, either biblical or non-biblical, a statement about a belief prevalent in our culture, and/or a focused question that is related to a specific experience. This should lead the participants to seek new or deeper insights and just as importantly to put those insights into practice through some concrete action or resolution. Theological reflection becomes easy over time.

[3] A specific way in which this might be done is to restructure marriage preparation programs. In addition, we might structure a special program for couples based on the RCIA model in which they are invited into a process of conversion. At the very least, there should be some effort at adult education with these couples with staff members and committed members of the parish community. Through warm, gentle relationships, we can begin to share with them our faith lives and invite them to be a part of it with us.

argue at length on behalf of a love that means being with others. When the Church thinks of saints, it thinks mostly of those who sacrifice themselves and not of those who nourish friendships such as marriages. Theologians who reflect on love commonly emphasize those New Testament texts that highlight *agapé*. They skip over the many texts that emphasize interpersonal relationships.... [I]n a word, communal life is neglected.[4]

In our preaching and teaching about God's love in the parish, we need to be careful to avoid a notion of friendship that does not challenge people into deeper community, working through hurts, sacrificing from one's substance and not only from one's excess, and embracing the challenge of the cross. These are the marks of a true Christian community living in God's friendship and sharing that gift with the world. From within this kind of community, moral discernment is well grounded upon a lived experience of our deepest identity in God.

III. INVITING OUR PEOPLE TO FRIENDSHIP WITH GOD

Every day we are making choices about whether to live as God's friends and grow in the Gospel life. Each choice we make is either deepening or dampening our friendship with God. Although there are many desires that pull at the human spirit, the deepest desire in the human heart is the desire for God. If we have a relationship with God through prayer, we have something that we can bring with us to the moral choices that we need to make. Another way of saying this is that if we are praying and are in touch with God, we will have some awareness of how the choices that face us will affect our relationship with God. This relationship throws light on the choices to be made. It is the value of this friendship with

---

[4] Vacek 280.

God that nuances and clarifies the moral choices that we face each day.

In the Middle Ages, St. Thomas Aquinas and St. Bonaventure argued about the evidence for the existence of God. St. Thomas wrote proofs about God's existence. He demonstrated that the world and all that is in it expresses the existence of a Supreme Being. Although St. Bonaventure did not disagree with this, he approached the question from another starting point. The Trinity was the centerpiece of St. Bonaventure's theology.[5] He wrote about the Trinity as being a network of relationships. The Father sent the Son. Jesus returned to the Father and sent the Holy Spirit. The Spirit moves and draws people to Christ, who in turn leads them back to the Father. St. Bonaventure suggested that the universe was filled with reflections of the Trinity. The very cosmos was about relationships, since relationships reflect the essence of God. Since this is so, St. Bonaventure argued that we exist only insofar as we are in relationship to God and to one another. His vision of the moral life emphasizes the cohesiveness among all that exists. Decisions that people make either enhance or detract from that cohesiveness. St. Bonaventure was less concerned about proving God's existence than he was about inviting people to live in relationship with the God who manifested Himself as Father, Son, and Holy Spirit. In his *Legenda Maior*, he used St. Francis of Assisi as a model to illustrate what this means.[6] St. Francis was one who lived out his awareness of our relationship with God who is Trinity and this awareness led him to love each and every creature in the universe. He treated them all with the greatest respect and dignity because

---

[5] St. Bonaventure and St. Thomas Aquinas debated the role of creation. St. Thomas saw creation in terms of causality. St. Bonaventure saw it as a reflection of the Trinity underscoring the essential role of relationships. For further detail, see Anthony Ciorra, *Everyday Mysticism* (New York: Crossroad, 1995) 99-100. An excellent explanation of the differences in thought between these two theologians can be found in Robert W. Shahan and Francis J. Kovach, eds., *Bonaventure and Aquinas: Enduring Philosophers* (Norman, OK: University of Oklahoma Press, 1976).

[6] St. Bonaventure, *The Life of St. Francis*, in *Bonaventure*, tr. Ewert Cousins (New York: Paulist Press, 1978).

everything mirrored God to him. In his example we find the foundation and principles for a moral life built upon relationships.

St. Thomas Aquinas also recognized the centrality of friendship with God as the core of the moral life. In his *Summa Theologiae*, he wrote, "Charity signifies not only love of God but also a certain friendship with God," which is "begun here in this life by grace, but will be perfected in the future life by glory."[7] He based his theology on St. John's definition of God: "God is Love" (1 Jn 4:8). Our friendship with God is an invitation through God's grace to accept that unconditional love or charity and, once received, to share it with others. The key is to understand that the invitation comes from God. St. Thomas writes:

> Charity, as we have said, is our friendship with God arising from our sharing in eternal happiness, which, according to St. Paul, is not a matter of natural goods but of gifts of grace: "The gift of God is eternal life" (Rm 6:23). Consequently charity is beyond the resources of nature, and therefore cannot be something natural or acquired by natural powers, since no effect transcends its cause. Hence we have it neither by nature nor as acquired by the Holy Spirit, who is the love of the Father and the Son; our participation in this love, as we have said earlier on, is creaturely charity itself.[8]

A. God's Grace: The Bridge to Charity

Charity stems from God's grace. God's grace, and God's grace alone, makes the lofty ideals of charity a possibility for us. God's

---

[7] Thomas Aquinas, *Summa Theologiae* I-II q. 65, a. 5. The text of the *Summa Theologiae* used is the Blackfriar's edition, ed. Thomas Gilby, O.P. (New York: McGraw-Hill Book Co., 1963-1969).

[8] *Summa Theologiae* II-II q. 23, a.1.

plan, offered through God's graciousness, is that we be in relationship with God and one another. Contemporary theories of moral development in one way or another affirm the necessity to contextualize moral growth within the framework of human relationships.[9] We would suggest that many of these theories find support in the Judeo-Christian tradition. This anthropology is expressed in the book of Genesis (Gn 1:26) in which the human person is said to be made in the image and likeness of God. If in fact God is Trinity, then the human person reflects that reality. Human beings find meaning and fulfillment to the degree that they embody the dynamic of the Trinity, which is sharing and self-giving. To sin is to choose not to be in relationship or to diminish the relationship in some way.

It becomes eminently clear as the Scriptures unfold that God is a Lover who invites people to share a covenant. It is God who frees the Israelites from slavery, constantly calling them away from those things that would entrap them and prevent them from realizing the fullness of their human potential. The image of a God who loves us and wants to free us reaches its peak in Jesus who announced that he had come that "we might have life, life to the very fullest" (Jn 10:10). He demonstrated this most clearly on the cross. This is the place where Jesus freed us and removed the barriers in our relationship with God and one another. On the cross Jesus is stretched between heaven and earth. He cries out to the Father with whom he is in relationship. At the same time, his outstretched arms embrace all humanity.

The cross, then, gives us a hint as to what it means to make

---

[9] Erik H. Erikson in his *Childhood and Society* (New York: W.W. Norton, 1963) teaches stages of human development that gradually move a person away from self-absorption towards commitment to other human beings. Lawrence Kohlberg, *The Philosophy of Moral Development*, vol. 1, *Essays on Moral Development* (San Francisco: Harper and Row, 1981), sees the process as one in which values of justice and right behavior towards others are internalized. This is the sign of maturity in his moral framework. Carol Gilligan, *In a Different Voice: Psychological Theory and Women's Development* (Cambridge, MA: Harvard University Press, 1982) responds to Kohlberg's theory by suggesting an ethics of care. In effect, she also affirms the importance of relationality.

decisions that will enhance relationships. Friendship with God and one another is the ultimate goal of the moral life. As Jesus said so well, "'You shall love the Lord your God with your whole heart, soul, and strength, and your neighbor as yourself.... These summarize both the law and the prophets'" (cf. Mt 22:37, 40). Friendship, however, is not possible without dying to self. The living out of our vocation to become like God, to reflect the Trinity is one that requires the cross for its fulfillment. This is indeed the way to holiness, the path to God. Our collective experience of God affirms that this call is invitational. The God who is love beckons us into a relationship with Himself. To accept this invitation is to embrace the cross. This self-giving will place us in relationship with every other human being. Indeed, our willingness to embrace the cross is the measuring rod of the authenticity of our moral choices.

B. Changed by Friendship

One of the ways that the spirituality of the cross has been poignantly articulated over centuries has been through the doctrine of the three ways. The stages of the three ways — purgative, illuminative, and unitive — provide a framework for growing in virtue and friendship with God and with one another.

In this framework, the spiritual journey begins with purgation. We must eliminate all those things that stand in the way of our spiritual growth. Vices must be purged and tendencies towards sin must be curbed through ascetical practices if we expect to grow spiritually. Many of the saints and mystics of past generations have advocated the purgative way as the starting point for our spiritual journey. St. Teresa of Avila in her *Interior Castle*, for example, teaches that the very first issue to be dealt with in our journey towards union with God is to let go of our sinfulness. Unless we are willing to do this, there is little hope of making any progress.

Once we have begun dealing with abandoning sin and vice, the next step is illumination. The word itself means to be enlightened. In this second step we are enlightened gradually, generally over a very long period of time, usually many years, by acquiring virtues. There is a conscious effort in this stage to acquire the virtues, beginning, one by one, to make them our own. This is the way to sanctity.

When we have been sufficiently purified and have replaced sin with virtue, then we are ready for union with God. This is the third and final step of the journey called the unitive way. This is sometimes, though not always, accompanied by extraordinary gifts such as ecstasy from the pure enjoyment of living in God's presence. People who reach this stage are occasionally given a foretaste of heaven, a glimpse, as it were, of the beatific vision. Deep faith, abiding hope, and especially self-sacrificing love, always characterize their lives.

Our understanding of this traditional doctrine of the three ways has developed along with our comprehension of theology, spirituality, and psychology. The dialogue among these disciplines has significantly contributed to a deepening of our appreciation of the spiritual life. Initially, most commentators on the doctrine of the three ways saw the steps as following one another. Today most reinterpret the doctrine of the three ways not as a ladder leading up to God but as a circle in which we are drawn to God at the center in a cyclical way — becoming ever more purified, ever more virtuous and ever more united to him who gives us the grace and help we need. In this view, we move in and out of the various stages many times throughout our lives. It has been the constant teaching of theologians and spiritual writers that growth in the spiritual life always stems from God's initiative. All is grace. Our role is to respond to that grace by accepting what God is offering.

With both of these approaches in mind, we would like to suggest an adaptation that would apply the doctrine of three ways to our contemporary world in a meaningful way for the average person. The underlying presupposition to this adaptation is that it is impossible to have a friendship with God and not to be changed by that friendship. Once in a relationship with God, we begin a lifelong process of being remade according to the Spirit of Love. The relationship is dynamic, not static. In addition, the change that we experience is authentic to the degree that it spills out into the world, especially in our relationships with others: "By their fruits you will know them" (cf. Mt 7:16). Our application of the doctrine of the three ways focuses, therefore, on our relationships with others and the world. In this proposed framework our relationship with God leads to a deeper relationship with other people. Conversely, our relationship with others leads to a fuller relationship with God. This approach embodies the challenge of the cross at its deepest level. The focus is no longer on our own progress but rather on the needs of others. We are no longer absorbed in self but rather absorbed in the arms of the Crucified One, whom we meet in the needs of people.

From this vantage point, the purgative way, the dying to self, begins by looking at the world and the culture in which we live. We begin by considering those aspects of the culture that we have absorbed and that conflict with Gospel values. The change or purgation that is called for is a radical one. We are called to change the way we have been living, to let go of the assumptions and goals that we might have held for many years. For example, our culture teaches that material success is important and that it usually comes only through competition with others. Achieving this success is supposed to bring us happiness. If we find that we have bought into this lie, to let go of it can be very painful, especially if we have built a life and a family around such goals. The purgation comes from learning to live differently than many people do in our society. The purgation comes from the rejection and ridicule that we might experience from others who are threatened by the truth of Gospel living.

The next step is the illuminative way. One of the virtues that clearly makes us counter-cultural is that of compassion. To be compassionate towards others is to do what Christ did. Compassion means "to suffer with." This is the virtue that is clearly the antithesis to an American individualism. Compassion draws us out of ourselves and our own needs and pulls us into the skin of others. It is the virtue by which we begin to feel what they feel. We become one with the poor, the sick and the abused in their suffering and pain.

Compassion naturally leads to the next step, which is solidarity with those who are suffering in any way. We are proposing solidarity as the unitive way. When we embrace those in need we embrace Christ himself. Union with God in this way is strong in the Christian spiritual tradition. For example, St. Martin of Tours found that the frozen beggar to whom he gave his cloak when he encountered him on the side of the road was Christ himself. St. Francis of Assisi found that, in embracing the leper whom he abhorred, he embraced Christ himself. Solidarity with others is solidarity or union with God.

No one is excluded because we are all sisters and brothers. In fact, to take this adaptation of the doctrine of the three ways seriously is to look for those in our society where most people would look last to find God and to find fulfillment. God lives with the poor. We meet the materially and spiritually poor every day of our lives. St. Augustine provides us with an interesting insight on this matter:

> Everyone must be loved equally. But when you cannot be of assistance to all, you must above all have regard for those who are bound to you more closely by some accident, as it were, of time, or place, or circumstance. For instance, suppose you had an abundance of something which you felt obliged to give to someone who did not have it, and were not able to give it to two persons. If two people came to you, neither of whom held precedence over the other, either because of want or any relationship to you, you could do nothing more just than decide by lot to which one you should give what you were unable to give to both. So, too, in the case of your fellowmen; since you cannot take care of all of them, you must decide by lot in proportion as each one can claim a closer connection with you at that time.[10]

---

[10] St. Augustine, "On Christian Instruction," *The Fathers of the Church: Writings of St. Augustine*, Vol. 4 (New York: Ludwig Schopp, 1950) 48.

St. Augustine's insight is about the specificity of sharing God's friendship with others in concrete ways. The "accidents" of who comes into our lives is an aspect of God's grace. In this adaptation of the three ways, the spiritual journey is about meeting concrete people along the way and responding in tangible ways. And there God is to be found. In coming to respond to the needs of others out of love of Christ, we are truly changed by this friendship with God.

IV. DISCERNMENT OF SPIRITS

The spiritual journey is one that requires a continuous choice to stay on the path that leads towards God. The decision to stay on that path, to continue to strive for communion with God and others, is one that demands ongoing discernment of spirits. Traditionally, discernment means deciding what promptings come from the Spirit of God and which come from the spirit of evil. Doing God's will, which is *to live the moral truth*, is the goal of Christian decision making. When we begin to look at concrete situations such as war, capital punishment, and sexual issues, it is not always easy to know what it is that God wants us to do. We need to develop the skills of discernment so that we might be sensitive to the movements of the Spirit of God.

The process of discernment is often a long and difficult one. Learning to be discerning persons is a lifetime task. Although moral teaching cannot be reduced to an exercise in authoritarianism, discernment must include knowledge of the truth as taught by the Church. Discernment is a process of personal discrimination and appropriation of those truths. Teaching people how to discern is based on the principle of the old adage, "Is it better to give a poor person a piece of fish or to teach him/her how to fish?" If people have been invited into a relationship with the Lord and have developed the skills of discernment, they will be more likely to make the choices that will keep that relationship alive and healthy. To teach people how to discern is to teach them how to fish. We give them a tool that they can carry with them throughout a lifetime and beyond.

As Catholics, we have a rich tradition regarding sage discernment and wise moral choices. Christian writers over the centuries have rooted their teachings in the Scriptures coupled with their own experience. St. Ignatius of Loyola is the classic example. After being wounded in the Battle of Pamplona, he lay in his bed in the family castle. He thought about his feelings for Lady Catherine. As he allowed his imagination to play itself out, he noticed that it gave him immediate satisfaction and pleasure but not long-term peace and happiness. He then began to read the Bible and the lives of the saints. He noticed that the challenge to live according to the principles of the Gospel and the example of the saints was initially frightening. However, in following those impulses, he noticed that he had a long-term sense of peace and deep satisfaction. In noticing these movements within himself, he began to develop the art of discernment. This art consisted in consciously noting those movements that bring us closer to God and those which distance us from him. Being aware of these movements points us in the direction of the choices that we should make to keep us in relationship with God.

In entering into the process of discernment, it is important always to begin with the Bible. This is God's revealed word to us. In it we find God calling the Israelites to be his own — a holy nation, a royal priesthood, a people set apart to form a social order based on a covenant in which they were to live together in community with God and one another. In this election by God, there is a specific call to holiness and justice. In reading Scripture, we derive insight into the way God deals with his people and that can give us an insight into how God deals with us. The themes of Scripture are clear and straightforward.[11] Parish staffs should provide

---

[11] We need to be careful of a biblical fundamentalism. The tools of the historical-critical method, among others, give us an approach to interpreting the Scriptures that is sound and sanctioned by the Church and most reputable scholars. A literal, fundamentalist approach to interpreting Scripture can lead to many faulty and harsh con-

adequate opportunities for Bible study. In so doing, it is important to strike the balance between solid academic study of the Scriptures and praying with the Bible. The two should go hand in hand.

Next, we are a Church with a very rich tradition. Looking to the tradition and teachings of the Church is an essential component in the discernment process. To ignore the Church and its teachings or to treat these casually indicates that one's discernment process is seriously flawed, if not totally invalidated. A critical problem in our day is that many people, especially young people, are losing touch with Church tradition. Things that pastoral ministers might take for granted, such as the principles of natural law or the social teachings of papal encyclicals, need to be introduced and explained clearly in our parishes. This is no easy task. Bulletin articles, adult education classes, and small faith communities are some of the ways in which this goal might be achieved. The homily is not usually the place to do this since it is to be a reflection on the Scriptures of the day. A possible suggestion is to take one or two minutes each Sunday as part of the announcements to explain a particular doctrine of the Church. This could be enhanced by a bulletin article and an adult education session following the liturgy.

In this whole process, it is important to take an approach to discernment that is holistic. All aspects of our personalities and our lives are in some way inter-connected. We need to be careful of compartmentalizing our lives. What we say in the Sunday liturgy is important for our lives for the rest of the week. The choices that we make during the week will impact what we bring back to the following week's liturgy. It is impossible to make a choice in one area that will not affect every other area of our lives. The impact

---

clusions. For an excellent article elaborating on the Vatican Biblical Commission stance on the issue of biblical interpretation and fundamentalism, cf. Joseph A. Fitzmyer, "The Interpretation of the Bible in the Church," *America* 169 (November 27, 1993): 12-15. The historical-critical method is not to be used in isolation from a life of prayer and faith. For further discussion on achieving this balance, cf. Luke Timothy Johnson, "So What's Catholic About It?" *Commonweal* 125 (January 16, 1998); 12-16; Gerald O'Collins and Daniel Kendall, *The Bible for Theology* (New York: Paulist Press, 1997); and Pontifical Biblical Commission, *The Interpretation of the Bible in the Church* (Roma: Libreria Editrice Vaticana, 1993).

of our choices is felt spiritually, emotionally, and even physically. Sexual morality, for example, is not only about physical actions. It is also about truth, intimacy, respect, and genuine happiness as opposed to fleeting pleasure. In creating our characters, the sexual decisions that we make affect all areas of our lives.

Every choice that we make contributes to the direction of our lives. To see choices isolated from a general direction or path that we are on is a serious mistake. As we continue to make choices on many issues, we are either becoming more dulled to or more attuned to God's plan for us.

In addition to a rational approach to understanding the tradition and the values it represents, it is also important to listen to our hearts. In a proper context, our feelings and impulses often tell us a great deal about what is right or wrong, and about what will best enable us to be in a proper relationship with God and the world.

The process of discernment should take place in the context of the community. In our culture many believe that religion should be something private. Some people think that their moral choices are simply a matter of personal opinion. We have seen that everything that we do impacts those around us. Individual choices affect the whole community. All of our choices should be made with an awareness of our relationship to the community. On the parish level we might encourage people to discuss their questions about choices with others in the community and even to seek advice or direction from qualified persons within the community.[12] Parish staff members should all acquire the skills necessary to teach discernment of spirits and to help people discern. This can be done through spiritual direction programs offered in most dioceses throughout the country. As part of this expertise, we would also underscore the importance of learning the skills of group spiritual

---

[12] For further reflections on the role of community and tradition, see Alisdair McIntyre, *After Virtue: A Study in Moral Theology* (Notre Dame, IN: University of Notre Dame Press, 1984) and Stanley Hauerwas, *A Community of Character* (Notre Dame, IN: University of Notre Dame Press, 1981).

direction. These are based on an excellent combination of the principles of the spiritual life, discernment of spirits, and group dynamic tools.

In engaging in this process in the parish, it is important to remember that we all are deeply influenced by our culture in our moral vision and values. Even committed Christians may not always be aware of the manner in which their choices are nuanced, however slightly, by the pull of the cultural environment. As part of the discernment process it is important to develop an awareness of these influences so that our moral choices will be free and in conformity with the values of the Gospel and our Catholic Christian tradition.

James Gustafson has written that the task of Christian ethics is to discern what God is enabling and requiring us to be and to do.[13] For some, it is difficult to understand the importance of discernment, how it works, and what discernment really means.[14] Richard Gula put his finger on this when he wrote:

> Virtuous moral living is like gourmet cooking. The Gourmet has recipe as a guide, but the gourmet cooks not by his or her head, but by taste. The decision of how much of what ingredient to add is led by a discerning taste rather than by a precisely defined recipe which can be followed blindly. Ordinary cooking follows the recipe

---

[13] James M. Gustafson, *Can Ethics Be Christian?* (Chicago: University of Chicago Press, 1975) 179.

[14] Some authors to consult on the topic of discernment are Jules Toner, S.J., *A Commentary on St. Ignatius' Rules for the Discernment of Spirits* (St. Louis: The Institute of Jesuit Sources, 1982); Toner, "The Deliberation that Started the Jesuits," *Studies in the Spirituality of Jesuits* 6:4 (June 1974); Toner, *The Experience of Love* (Washington, DC: Corpus Books, 1968); Toner, "A Method for Communal Discernment of God's Will," *Studies in the Spirituality of Jesuits* 3:4 (September 1971); and, Toner, *Discerning God's Will* (St. Louis: Institute of Jesuit Sources, 1991). Karl Rahner has significantly influenced all thinking about Ignatian discernment in his essay "The Logic of Concrete Individual Knowledge in Ignatius Loyola," in *Dynamic Element in the Church* (New York: Herder and Herder, 1964) 84-170. A readable and well-respected work on discernment is Thomas Green, S.J., *Weeds Among the Wheat* (Notre Dame, IN: Ave Maria Press, 1984).

exactly, even to the point of leveling the teaspoon with a scraper to make sure the measurement is exactly what the recipe prescribes. The resulting meals are adequate to keep one nourished, but they are not always exciting and they do not reflect the personal taste of the cook in the way a gourmet meal does. The gourmet version of the moral life does not dispense with the recipes of moral norms, but the moral gourmet is not so bound by the recipe that he or she would not adjust according to taste. Discernment is what helps the gourmet make the proper adjustments. So if the moral life is going to be a personal response to one's hearing the call of God in this instance, moral discernment of spirits is indispensable.[15]

Discernment is the bridge linking the moral life to the spiritual life. Discernment is a listening with the ears of faith to the inner movements (i.e., feelings, attractions, hungers, impulses, resistances, etc.) of the spirit. Methods and traditions of discernment are geared at helping a person to be faithful in his or her response to God.

Jules Toner in his writings makes a distinction between the discernment of spirits and the discernment of God's will. He suggests that discovering God's will is a step beyond discernment of spirits in that it is concerned with specific actions or moral behaviors. He underscores the critical nature of trying to find God's will in the environment of contemporary freedom and personal responsibility. In the current cultural atmosphere people are making their own choices and not simply blindly obeying Church rules and regulations. Instead, they often give blind obedience to the popular culture and its "traditions." Understanding discernment of spirits is even more crucial in this kind of contemporary environment. What follows are some practical guidelines for teaching people about the importance of discernment so that they can make mature and *faith*-centered moral choices.

---

[15] Richard M. Gula, S.S., *Reason Informed By Faith* (New York: Paulist Press, 1989) 315.

A. Understanding Discernment of Spirits

Discernment is really a straightforward process. To discern is to notice what we are feeling and thinking. It is the habit of distinguishing movements of God from movements of our ego. Discernment is an art that we must cultivate. Slowing down and learning how to pay attention to what is going on within and around us are the essential components for discerning the spirits. After awhile discernment becomes second nature to us. For one who practices discernment and lives in friendship with God, the distinction of what is of God and what is not becomes easier to determine over time.

There are many spirits at work. There is the spirit of God, the spirit of the world, the spirit of evil, the spirit of other people, and our own spirit. Discernment at its most basic level consists of recognizing differences. These differences are not always between good and evil. Feeling good or peaceful is not necessarily a sign that something is of God. In fact it is possible that there can be experiences of harmony and tranquility that not only do not open us to God but rather close off that relationship.

B. What Are These Different Movements?

Because there are several different spirits that abound, there are different movements or pulls that a person can experience. On the one hand, we can be moved to make certain choices that will lead us closer to God. On the other hand, there can be counter-movements that present choices that will dampen our friendship with God.

When St. Ignatius reflected on these various movements or tugs that would draw us away from God, he attributed these to the devil or evil spirits. Another way of expressing this reality is to say that the enemy is anything that interferes with or pulls us away from our relationship with God. St. Ignatius learned to notice the immediate experience of a choice as compared to its long-term effect. Ultimately the issue is learning to notice what brings life to our relationship with God and what deadens or dulls it.

All serious Christians will have to deal with discerning the spirits as their relationship with God develops. What we are proposing is that discernment needs to be learned and nurtured. In this context, the basic counter-movement away from God is the urge not to notice, not to pay attention. In our culture it is especially difficult to become discerning people because of the many voices that filter in through the media and the many venues that other technologies have opened up for us. In addition, the pace of life is accelerating at an alarming pace, primarily due to economic reasons and concerns. Our culture does not nurture or support the value of developing a discerning spirit regarding what is right or wrong. Ours is a culture that is so focused on economic goals that the moral life is often viewed as irrelevant. In such an environment the goal is self-*fulfillment* and not the self-*transcendence* of the cross.

C. The Role of the Director

Our tradition uses the word "director" to describe those who help us discern and guide us in our spiritual growth. A spiritual director can be anyone who is competent to give insight into prayer and decision making. We are not speaking here of spiritual direction in the strict sense. Although we should encourage people who are ready to seek spiritual direction, we should not limit our notion of spiritual direction to the classical one-on-one relationship.

In the broader sense, spiritual direction can happen within the liturgy. For those who participate regularly in the liturgy there is an evolving and consistent message in its annual cycle. As we have seen, the liturgy also can be a graced moment in which one is touched and moved by God. This was true for many of the saints and mystics. The liturgy is a place where God communicates with us. God communicates in symbolic, often tangible and human ways. The Spirit of God touches us in the liturgy. What we need to bring is an open, listening spirit.

Spiritual direction can happen between friends. Friends who are focused on God can help one another pay attention to various movements and directions in their lives. Again, this was true of the saints. St. Francis and St. Clare, St. Francis de Sales and St. Jane de Chantal were spiritual directors for one another. They advised, challenged, and helped one another in their relationship with God.

We already noted the growing phenomenon of group spiritual direction. This is a model that can be very practical and effective in the parish setting. This approach is based on the "support group" model. The person leading the group would have to have a knowledge of theology, spirituality, spiritual direction, and some basic counseling and group management skills. In the interaction and sharing, all in the group would be helping one another on the spiritual journey.

In spiritual direction, one person serves the other as director or facilitator of their spiritual life. It is not a relationship based on directive commands or obedience, but rather one of companionship on the spiritual journey. In this setting, there are regular meetings in which the directee shares his or her prayer life and relationship with God and the director listens, clarifies, and challenges.

In the model mentioned above, the role of the director is to help the person notice their desire for something more, to keep looking at God. The director helps the person to stay with the movement towards life and always to make those choices that will help the directee to opt for and grow more deeply in relationship with God. The director is in a privileged position to reflect on the moral choices that the directee needs to make, and can point out what choices are deepening the relationship with God and which are detracting from that relationship.

D. The Relationship between Prayer and Discernment

Prayer is the heart of the spiritual direction relationship. The director is essentially listening to what happens in the directee's prayer. Without prayer there can be no discernment. There is little to discuss if a person is not praying. However, even if a person is not praying, he or she is still making decisions. These decisions may or may not be good. In either case, the decisions or choices are not made from the context of their relationship with God. Other factors, such as common sense, expediency, personal satisfaction, etc., are what guide people who are not praying. This is not to say that they are necessarily making bad decisions. It is to say, however, that they have made the decision not to be in a close relationship with God. And, as a result, they do not have the strength of that relationship to bring to their decision-making processes.

A challenge for anyone who is a director is to be aware of a human tendency to discontinue a dialogue with God prematurely. In our interpersonal relationships, oftentimes we do this because we are afraid, hurt, angry, or bored. Blandness in speaking of the Lord can imply a desire to keep God at an emotional distance. Maybe the person just doesn't want to tell God what he or she is feeling. Other times a person may simply be unaware that there are feelings to be expressed.

A director may be helpful by asking, "Do you remember the last time that prayer was exciting or interesting for you? What were you talking about?" The director might pick up on what the person was talking about to God and ask, "What happened to that topic?" A person needs to go back to that topic, otherwise his or her prayer will be dull.

Prayer will be boring if we are not being ourselves before God. We can posture before God when there is an area in our life that we are not dealing with. Directors need to be careful not to forget that often difficulties in prayer are due to the suppression of important attitudes and feelings. Thus, we should be careful not to accept on face value statements like, "I didn't have time to pray," or "I pray on the run." The director should help the directee get to the reasons why they are making such choices. The task of the director is always to challenge the directee to deepen their relationship with God and to make good moral decisions based on that relationship.

E. Deciding What Comes from God

The core questions underneath all that we have said are, "What is God saying? Where is God in this particular situation?" It is difficult to know for sure what comes from God and what does not. We need to be careful of being too glib about declaring what comes from God. We should be careful of anyone who is self-appointed proclaimer of God's will.

Having noted these cautions, it is certainly possible to have some sense of where God is leading us. This is based on the assumption that God is trying to communicate with us. We know this from the teaching of the Scriptures and from over four thousand years of experience in the Judeo-Christian tradition. We have come to know God as One who communicates with us and has a definite plan for our personal and communal lives.

Given this reality, we can measure our experience of God against the experience of others as recorded in the Scriptures or our tradition. It can also be helpful to compare a current experience with a previous experience of God. We can get a picture and some idea of what God is like. There is a consistency in God. If my experience is leading me in a direction away from the consistency of God's revelation, then chances are that this movement is not from God. For example, a person might have an especially intense experience of God's unconditional love while reading the Scriptures or participating in the liturgy. It is clear to the person that this is a movement that comes from the Spirit of God. The experience of God's love is rather consistent for this person. One day the person suddenly feels that God wants to punish him or her and that salvation is very uncertain. When this latter experience is measured against the consistency of the experience of God's love and mercy, it should be clear that this movement is not from God but rather from some other spirit. Again, the director's task is to help the directee to see these patterns and to be in touch with the various movements.

F. Signs that We Are on the Right Track

A sense of peace is often a sign that a person is on the right track. Oftentimes people think that, because they feel "peace" about something, it is a sign of God's action or approval of their choice. What is this thing that we call peace? We would propose that it is not necessarily a feeling. The core of what we mean by peace is a sense of inner freedom that results from openness to God and willingness to respond to God. For example, the Gospel portrayal of Christ at the Last Supper is filled with many different emotions, many of which were far from peaceful. In fact, he was filled with inner turmoil and deep anguish.

If we are choosing to live in relationship with God, even in the midst of the most painful feelings there can be an inner freedom that comes from the assurance of living out this relationship. This is certainly what Jesus experienced throughout his passion and agony. This is Shalom, a deep sense of well-being even amidst trials. For those living out a relationship with God, there is a core sense of integrity and well-being that nothing in this world can take away (Romans 8).

Coming from another vantage point, peace can also mean the absence of strong feelings (e.g., fear, anger, disappointment, etc.). It is natural to want to withdraw from such feelings because they are uncomfortable. However, God might be in such feelings, moving the person to deeper action or challenging the person to new growth. In such instances there might not be a surface sense of peace but rather a deeper sense of integrity in doing God's will. There may be nothing nice about the surface feeling but the deeper attitude is one of well-being and overwhelming freedom.

St. Ignatius of Loyola in the *Spiritual Exercises* is deeply concerned about the person who is consistently unruffled. There is something not right about this kind of individual. If an individual does not experience ups and downs in prayer, then he or she must ask if significant experiences or painful feelings are being avoided. God might very well be in these experiences that are far from peaceful. Dealing with them can cause great conflict but result in ultimate freedom and true peace.

When we speak of moral issues, there are choices that are closed to us. Depending on the issue and circumstances, there may or may not be leeway. Bringing a moral choice to prayer does not suggest a rigid, cold standing before God to receive an immediate mandate for implementation of a moral precept. The material for prayer is the turbulence, rebellion, and emotional uncertainties connected with the choice. The person goes to prayer to be in relationship with God precisely in the midst of these feelings. The end result if one has truly prayed might be healing, new resolve, or the courage to carry out an action that might be especially painful or difficult. Prayer, however, does not necessarily take away the painful struggle to make the right choice. The immediate effect of a morally correct choice might be agonizing. Directors need to encourage people not to be afraid of this darkness. God is there and in the end there is light. Oftentimes prayer calls us to a deeper faith in making choices that require a dying to self. The vision that the director must keep before the directee is that "unless the grain of wheat falls to the earth and dies, it remains just a grain of wheat. But if it dies it will bear much fruit" (Jn 12:24). This is the experience of the paschal mystery that comes from embracing the cross.

Scripture is quite clear in giving us measuring rods for examining the choices we make. St. Paul writes, "The fruit of the Spirit is love, joy, peace, patient endurance, kindness, generosity, faith, mildness, and chastity" (Gal 5:22). The presence of these qualities has become further evidence that we have made choices that are from the urgings of the Holy Spirit. The difficulty again is how to measure these. For example, relief at making a decision can look like the peace of the Spirit, witless enthusiasm can look like joy, and apathy sometimes resembles patience. Only over time ("by their fruits will you know them") and by observing behavior is it ultimately possible to determine what actually stems from God's will for us.

G. What Actually Is God's Will?

The problem is that sometimes when people speak of doing God's will they seem to imply that there is a blueprint in heaven. Their goal then becomes to get a peak at the blueprint to find out what they are supposed to do. This approach oftentimes carries a sense of urgency or panic to find out what the blueprint has to show us.

This represents an image of God that is static and non-relational. This suggests a God who is stoic and computer-like in dealing with us. The God who wants to invite us into a relationship disappears into the static God who has a plan that we have to try to unravel.

Simply put, our relationship with God should help us make the choices that need to be made. The key question is: "What choice is going to best keep me in relationship with God and make this relationship continue to grow?" Analogous to the marital relationship, often a couple only has to look at each other to make the choices that are healthy and consistent with their relationship. The choices that we make should be life-giving for our relationship to God and our relationships with others.

The Enemy of our life does not want us to be in relationship to God. We can be moved to pray and to follow the Lord. At the same time we can be moved to not pray and walk away from God. This latter counter-movement is a resistance to change and growth. This is evil, i.e., anything that interferes with the relationship. This is the fundamental choice that needs to be made. Which movement will we follow? This choice will ultimately impact our moral behavior and action.

Discernment is not some esoteric or unusual experience. Once attuned to the movements of the Spirit, it becomes quite natural and even easy to know what choices and behaviors should be followed. Marriage is the best analogy. Two people deeply in love for many years often no longer need to speak their thoughts and desires to one another. They are so attuned to one another's spirit that they just know what the other wants or needs. The longer we choose to accept God's invitation to be in relationship with him, the more we are naturally inclined to know what is coming from God's spirit and what is not.

The questions about moral choices should be the material of our prayer and should energize our relationship with God. Obviously, we need to encourage people to make the right choices. These choices should be made in the context of their relationship with God. Again, our fundamental message is an invitation to a relationship with God. While we encourage people to make the right choices, we must also be clear that God's love is not dependent on making the right choices. God's love and desire to be in relationship with us is independent of our choices, feelings, and thoughts. Even if we choose not to be in relationship to God, God still loves us and wants to be in relationship with us.

Finally, discernment is not magic. It demands that we live life with self-awareness and a deep sense of prayer. A life of discipleship is at the core of discernment. Maybe the reason why so many in our culture make choices contrary to the values of the Gospel is that they do not have a relationship of discipleship with the Lord. Discernment has to do with staying in that relationship and making the choices that will keep that relationship alive and well.

> Although discernment does not yield the certitude we may like to have in directing our lives through moral choices in complex circumstances, it does stimulate our desire to find God in all things and to be mindful of being subject to the presence and governing action of God. Discernment does not consign us to discontent or moral paralysis; instead as faith increasingly informs reason, we live more consciously, freely, and faithfully in the service of God, treating all things as relative to God and choosing all our actions in response to God. This, in brief, is the culmination of the moral life lived according to reason informed by faith.[16]

---

[16] Gula 328.

V. CONCLUSION

The images most used in Scripture for God are spouse, parent, and friend. In the Gospel of John, Jesus says that he no longer calls us servants, he calls us friends (Jn 15:15). This is the most powerful image of God. To say that we are invited into friendship with God means that all barriers are removed. We are invited to the same intimacy with the Father that Jesus has. This is the most essential principle of the spiritual life and one of the most important teachings of the entire New Testament.

Parish staff members are people who are living out a relationship of discipleship. They are Jesus' friends and followers. From this primary relationship they are called to be community with one another. It is to this community of friendship that they invite the rest of the parish. If the staff is truly centered on Jesus, the way they relate to one another and the parish community will in itself be inviting. Their actions will speak louder than words. People will be drawn to want to share in the warmth and support of this kind of community: "See how these Christians love one another" (Jn 13:34-35).

Parish staff members invite others to share in this relationship with the Lord and one another through word and example. Once people come into the community, it is the staff's primary mission to help people develop and deepen these relationships. One of the ways that this happens is by putting people in touch with the Church's moral norms through the community's wisdom tradition and the Scriptures. *The staff should be a discerning fraternity, who in turn teach the parish the skills of discernment so that the whole community will make those choices that will keep them in relationship with God and one another.*

CHAPTER FOUR

PERSONAL ETHICS: ISSUES IN MARRIAGE AND FAMILY

Ethics is primarily about the development of moral character. Our moral character then influences the way we arrive at moral judgments. Our characters are formed by what we pay attention to, by what we love. For the Christian, the center of religious conversion is a falling in love with God in Christ. Thus our characters are formed by our loving attention to Christ. And so, Christians reason out of a mind and heart given over to God in love. *Wanting* to have one's mind and heart affected by Christ is what typifies a Christian desire to be good. In this chapter we will approach the moral issues of marriage and family from the perspective of the virtues needed to assist in correct judgment. These virtues are necessarily, but not exclusively, founded upon a love for God in Christ, therein imbuing in faith the entire regimen of ethical deliberation and moral behavior. We see that our entire ethical life is based upon the reorienting of our love toward objects worthy of our dignity as persons. Certainly, God is such a worthy object of love, as is one's spouse. If the parish could assist us to form consciences alert to our fundamental relatedness to God and other persons, ethical judgment would center upon what is truly essential.

I. MARRIAGE PREPARATION

A recent study by Creighton University found that Church-sponsored marriage preparation programs are generally successful in helping couples make a Christian vision of marriage their own. It concluded that education about marriage should not be limited to pre-marital education but, for highest effectiveness, become established in parish adult education forums. The study showed that the participants found educational material on the Church's moral values to be helpful.[1] Moreover, it also concluded that the formation team must have and must communicate to participants their high expectations regarding the couples' appropriation of Church doctrine. It became clear that if the presenters take the importance of marriage formation seriously, the participating engaged couples will rise to meet those expectations.[2]

This study is important because it affirms the Church's long-time practice of sponsoring marriage preparation programs. It also highlights the need for instructors in these programs to know the theological and sacramental meaning of Christian marriage, and to communicate this to couples. Marriage preparation teams cannot be content simply to teach communication and fiscal responsibility skills. The study found that engaged couples are open to receive the Church's teaching on values during marital formation, and thus the pastoral team may want to be bolder in specifically evangelizing and catechizing the participants. A couple's preparation for Christian marriage can become a time of grace, a time to be affected by the Holy Spirit, and, if need be, a time to embrace a moral conversion.

When training couples to facilitate marriage preparation classes, it is always helpful to give them opportunities to embrace objectivity and prudence that they may communicate Church

---

[1] Center for Marriage and Family, *Marriage Preparation in the Catholic Church: Getting it Right* (Omaha, NE: Creighton University, 1995) 102. For the Pope's teaching on marriage, see John Paul II, *The Theology of the Body: Human Love in the Divine Plan* (Boston: Pauline Books and Media, 1997).

[2] Center for Marriage and Family 48.

teaching in a positive and affirming manner. By saying this we are not recommending that cultural criticism of Catholic moral doctrine be ignored or impugned; it is to be engaged and its arguments addressed. However, the engaged couples are owed correct teaching within an ambiance of respect and enthusiasm. This is particularly true in two areas. First, the issues concerning reproduction are so volatile within our society that careful and explicit doctrinal formation on issues such as *in vitro* fertilization, sterilization, surrogate motherhood, abortion, the RU 486 pill, and artificial contraception would enhance team readiness. Certainly not all of these issues need to be formally presented to the engaged couples, but informal questions regarding them may arise. We believe it is especially vital to discuss the issue of gender roles within marriage in light of Catholic teaching, which emphasizes equality and mutuality. The U.S. Catholic bishops expressed it this way:

> True equality, understood as mutuality, is not measuring out tasks... or maintaining an orderly schedule. It thrives at a much deeper level where the power of the Spirit resides.... Mutuality is really about sharing power and exercising responsibility for a purpose larger than ourselves.[3]

Second, the issue of consumerism is an appropriate addition to marriage preparation programs in light of current advertising trends, which spur consumption for reasons other than and beyond authentic physical and psychological needs. Consumerist mentalities can threaten family economic security, family intimacy and quality time as well as stir anger and dissension between spouses as they vie with one another for use of limited funds. As with sexuality, the topic of consumer habits needs to be approached with prudence and sensitivity. Defenses can go up rather quickly if this

---

[3] U.S. Bishops, *Follow the Way of Love* (Washington, DC: United States Catholic Conference, 1994) 20. John Paul II, *Mulieris Dignitatem* (On the Dignity and Vocation of Women), Apostolic Letter, August 15, 1988. See *Origins* 18 (October 3, 1988): 261+.

topic is raised in a judgmental way. The Church does not condemn wealth. It does, however, warn of the degrading effects of wealth on persons who identify themselves with what they own. Seen in this way, consumerism is a religious issue because it threatens to undermine our dependence upon God. It strikes at our ability to trust and draw our life's purpose from God. In wealthy parishes this topic appears to need much more emphasis in marriage preparation courses than the traditional lesson on how to manage a family budget and checkbook. In economically poorer parishes, the specter of consumerism is present not in persons actually identifying themselves with the things they own, but in identifying themselves by the things they lack. It is the opposite side of the same coin. As Americans we swim in a consumerist culture. The Church's ambivalent attitude toward wealth will be discussed in more detail below, as will sexual ethics.

The need for catechesis in the sacrament of marriage is crucial. In it we will need to strike a balance between good conscience formation in Christian truths and the skills of social analysis. This social analysis is key to understanding an American culture within which many Catholics have been formed to criticize Christian values rather than appropriate them. Even many Catholics regard the conscience as predominantly *private*. Approaches to successfully evangelizing and catechizing persons into a communal notion of the development of conscience requires vital pastoral skills. An education in morality within the parish affirms the judgments of conscience as subjectively absolute but at the same time calls people to discern if that same conscience has been properly formed. Ought we not try to expose parishioners to unknown sources of formation such as many of the social teachings of the Church? Ought we not challenge our parishioners to become more "open" and "inclusive," and to look again at previously rejected sources of ecclesial formation such as *Humanae Vitae* or *On Euthanasia*?[4]

---

[4] Pope Paul VI, *Humanae Vitae* (The Regulation of Birth) in Claudia Carlen, I.H.M., *The Papal Encyclicals 1958-1981*, vol. 5 (McGrath Publishing Company, 1981) 223-236. See also Congregation for the Doctrine of the Faith, *Declaration On Euthanasia* (Washington, DC: USCC, 1980).

To do moral education in the context of marriage requires a deeper development in the virtue of listening to God and to one's spouse, a skill we discussed above in Chapters Two and Three. If the skill of listening is mastered, then one can be more open to previously rejected or unknown sources of wisdom. To master listening is to master a key disposition in moral living. We will look at this virtue in the context of prayer and communication.

II. PRAYER AND COMMUNICATION BETWEEN SPOUSES

The Catholic Church takes marriage very seriously. It requires a certain level of spiritual maturity on the part of the spouses so that they can embrace God as well as one another within their loving commitment. This commitment is fueled by grace, and quite plainly its success, measured in the fidelity of the spouses to one another, depends upon the couple drawing strength from grace to love one another joyfully "unto death." Our culture now affirms the standard of serial monogamy rather than "until death do us part." The Church's theology of marriage, however, still affirms the possibility, in grace, of commitment until death.

The art of communication is an indispensable key to a faithful marriage. It is as necessary as learning how to override one's own ego and its relentless needs in order to enter the needs or the presence of another.[5] From these graced skills come many fruits, including patience (the ability to suffer *for* another) and compassion (the ability to suffer *with* another). These virtues can be practiced, confirmed, and strengthened in two primary ways: actual communication with one's spouse, and actual communication with God. These two forms of communication are distinct and should retain their distinction. We do not think it wise to "collapse" one's

---

[5] See Gilbert Meilander, *The Theory and Practice of Virtue* (Notre Dame, IN: University of Notre Dame Press, 1984). Also Benedict Ashley, O.P., *Living the Truth in Love* (New York: Alba House, 1996) 34-38.

love for God into one's love for spouse, or vice versa.[6] By attending to both distinctively it will be found that the presence of one will effortlessly interpenetrate the other. While praying, my spouse and his or her needs will come to my heart, and in my loving communication with my spouse the presence of God will come to mind and I will praise God for such a union.

What, then, is prayer in the context of marriage? We all look for perfection, and much of our seeking for God is masked in our unremitting search for the perfect, "the more." If we expect this desire to be fulfilled in our spouse we will be disappointed. No human can satisfy our need for the divine. Perhaps in marriage preparation more emphasis has to be placed on the fact that whomever one marries, he or she will be imperfect. "How do I live with a spouse who has sinned against me?" Obviously this requires a prior formation in the virtues of forgiveness, courage, and self-esteem. Many of us have a sense of raw justice, not forgiveness — when sinned against, we tend to want to "get even." Most of the time this is acted out in unconscious ways. We do this by giving our spouse the "silent treatment" or by immediately drawing attention to his/her faults. Being formed in the likeness of Jesus, we can approach the behavior of our spouses in a different way. We are not marrying perfect people nor do we have to become perfect, but we do have to grow in love and in the virtues of forgiveness. Prayer in the context of marriage is undertaken with the disposition and expectation of being affected by Christ, and in turn of being an occasion of grace for one's spouse. We can only be so if we have allowed the virtues of Christ to penetrate our hearts. We want to listen to God in prayer so that we might be molded according to the truth of Christ, and then live out that truth in the presence of our spouse.

Listening to God in prayer bears fruit in our sacramental love. It is vital to invite engaged couples to begin marriage with an ex-

---

[6] Edward C. Vacek, "The Eclipse of Love for God," *America* 174:8 (March 9, 1996): 13-16.

plicit consciousness of its theological meaning, because faith tells us that in marriage the love we have for self, spouse, and God becomes the prime reality within which we receive salvation. That is why marriage is a sacrament. It is a commitment, for those called to it, within which one explicitly knows that his or her salvation is being worked out. The prayer of marriage is simply the deepening of the couple's desire to be affected by the love of God. In this way, this skill of listening and of being vulnerable to the presence of another becomes the mutually enriching route to a good marriage and a good relationship with God. Of course, a vision of marriage based upon listening to one another and to God is more fully received and understood as the fruit of *many years* of loving and forgiving.

Pastoral Suggestions

Two things can be done in the pastoral realm to assist couples with shared prayer:

1. Preach and teach on the meaning and methods of prayer. Specifically invite couples to any forums where prayer will take place and/or is taught. The specificity of the invitation might lead couples to consider their own prayer life together and as individuals.
2. In marriage preparation processes, emphasize the listening quality of prayer and exhort the couples to see the skills of prayer as the skills needed to be a moral presence to one another (attentiveness, patience, respect for otherness, etc.). We do less evil to one who has been taken into the listening heart.[7]

Married life is very difficult today because so much conspires to take the spouses' focus off one another and their love for God.

---

[7] *Gaudium et Spes* (Pastoral Constitution on the Church in the Modern World) 62. *Vatican Council II: The Conciliar and Post Conciliar Documents*, ed. Austin Flannery (Wilmington: Scholarly Resources, 1975). See also Sylvia Fleming Crocker, "Prayer as a Model of Communication," *Pastoral Psychology* 33 (Winter, 1984): 83-92.

The cultural supports needed to help couples listen to one another are flimsy. Society rather fosters our preoccupation with activity and seems to ignore the value of that quiet which is necessary to facilitate both spousal communication and prayer. In the dissolution of a relationship many sins can be committed. The breaking of one's word, the marriage vow, is itself a very serious matter. Even so, one can repent of the sins involved in any divorce and move on in life, pledging to cooperate again with God's grace. It is the goal of the Church's marriage ministry to forestall some of the potential causes of divorce through education, counseling, and spirituality. Communication between spouses is, of course, not a cure-all for the high divorce rate in our culture, but it can help to minimize ignorance of self, fiancé(e), or spouse. If this ignorance is reduced, some impending marriages that are based on a superficial knowledge of the other may rightfully never take place, or it may, at least, present an opportunity for healing. Anyone who has worked in marriage preparation considers it a sign of success when a couple not ready for marriage breaks their engagement as a result of knowledge learned through the preparation process.

To close on a very practical point, may we recommend that those in the parish who preside at worship truly utilize the times *built into* liturgy for quiet. In this way, and through appropriate catechesis, parish worship can whet the appetite for, and discipline the will toward, a silence rich in the possibility of intimacy. All that the couple has to give to the community hinges upon their meeting God in their mutually listening hearts. Without this achieved intimacy, each spouse draws only upon his or her own limited resources. The glory of marriage in Christ, however, is that one's identity is realized in the giving of the self over to the beloved. This kind of self-giving is essential to genuine marital communication just as it is in any deeply personal prayer.

III. MONEY AND CONSUMERISM

The Hebrew and Christian traditions are ambivalent about the possession and use of money and property. The Scriptures and the Church Fathers are very suspicious of wealth, recognizing it as dangerous to one's moral progress. St. Paul even went so far as to say that "the love of money is the source of all evil" (1 Tm 6:10) due to the temptation of greed.[8] But the Church has never taught that being rich is immoral *per se*. What Catholic moral tradition *has* taught is that the rich must share their wealth with those in need and that those who are able to support themselves and their families must do so and not burden society because of their laziness or moral turpitude.

The question is complicated, however, by our recognition of what has been called "social sin." It is an expression which refers to the sinful choices of individuals — rich and poor — that become part of the very social fabric of a culture, manifesting themselves in such patterns of behavior as racism, sexism, ageism, "group think" and other forms of biases. Some people are rich because they use power to keep those more vulnerable from economically participating in society. On the other hand, some people can compound their material poverty with attitudes of helplessness which keep them forever "victims" of a fate "imposed" on them by those they blindly hate. Nevertheless, because of the power given to the wealthy by their riches, they must be ever on guard against the temptation to exploit the powerless. The harshest judgments in all of Scripture are reserved for those with wealth. The "preferential option for the poor" espoused by the Second Vatican Council was preached and practiced by God from the very beginning.[9]

---

[8] Luke 12:16-21, 18:24-30. See also St. Augustine, "[T]he superfluities of the rich are the necessities of the poor. When you possess what is above your needs, you possess the goods of others," as quoted in Peter Phan, *Social Thought* (Wilmington, DE: Michael Glazier, 1984) 197.

[9] Stephen Pope, "Proper and Improper Partiality and the Preferential Option for the Poor," *Theological Studies* 54 (1993): 242-271.

Marriage is profoundly influenced by the social and economic situation of the nation. In marriage, two people, while remaining equal yet distinct, establish a household based on a shared economy. Each spouse has his or her own selfish tendencies, and still the objective needs of the family have to be met. Surviving economically as a family despite the many temptations to greed, laziness, or the exploitation of others, sometimes including one's own spouse and children, is an achievement that is sorely underrated. Recently, official Church teaching has emphasized the moral danger of personal and familial greed appearing in the form of consumerism, "keeping up with the Joneses."[10]

Consumerism is a lifestyle wherein one derives the major part of his or her self-worth from the pursuit of buying and owning "things." The "sin" of consumerism is found in seeking to acquire *things* as an end in themselves.[11] How one spends money, and for what, is a perennial source of friction in marriages. If we could assist couples in setting out a clear plan for spending in light of the purposes of their marriage, then perhaps consumerist behavior could be lessened. This assistance invites the couple to question how they use money to facilitate the moral ends of marriage.

We do not come together in a Christian marriage simply to fulfill the needs of merchandisers and marketers — we come together in Christ to love, and serve the needs of one another, our children and the wider community. What material goods do we need to live such a life? Consumerism can only be eradicated by replacing it with another spirituality. To categorize consumerism as a spirituality is to say that it takes on the dynamism of a religion: giving meaning to one's life and forming character. Keeping the Christian meaning of marriage as primary illuminates a spiritual alternative to consumerism.

Pope John Paul II has written extensively on the subject of

---

[10] John Paul II, *Sollicitudo rei socialis* (On Social Concern) (Washington, DC: USCC, 1987) 28.

[11] See James Donohue et al., eds., *Religion, Ethics and the Common Good* (Mystic, CT: Twenty-Third Publications, 1996).

consumerism, which he aptly describes as "artificial consumption."[12] This valuable expression captures the essence of consumerism in its endless quest to accumulate material goods, *super* accumulation really. And since much of what we accumulate is needless waste, discarding become easier once the product's initially-seen usefulness has been replaced by the brightness of a product that is "new and improved."[13]

> It is not wrong to want to live better; what is wrong is a style of life which is presumed to be better when it is directed toward *having* rather than *being,* and which wants to *have* more, not in order to *be* more but in order to spend life in enjoyment as an end in itself. It is therefore necessary to create life-styles in which the quest for truth, beauty, goodness and communion with others for the sake of common growth are the factors which determine consumer choices....[14]

In deciding how to spend their money, married couples should ask themselves whether or not their consumer choices assist in promoting communion with their spouse for the sake of common growth. This is more interesting and complex than simply buying something because they have the resources or out of impulse. A firm identity of purpose is the best defense against the powerful social and media forces conspiring to make us all live beyond our means.

To be converted from flagrant consuming habits is very difficult as reports on American credit card debt bear out.[15] However, conversion is possible in the context of grace, as a couple either

---

[12] John Paul II, *Centesimus Annus* (On the Hundredth Anniversary of *Rerum Novarum*) (Washington, DC: USCC, 1991) 36. See also *Sollicitudo rei socialis* 28.

[13] See John Kavanaugh, *Following Christ in a Consumer Society Still: The Spirituality of Cultural Resistance,* rev. ed. (Maryknoll, NY: Orbis Books, 1991).

[14] *Centesimus Annus* 36, emphasis added.

[15] See P. Keating, "How to Avoid Being Swamped by Your Credit Card Debt," *Money* 24 (March, 1995): 40ff.

begins their marriage or "begins again" on the firm footing of knowing that the spiritual purpose of marriage is the common quest for holiness. This is not simply a reminder of a basic premise of the faith, but also one of the most powerful antidotes we have to the persuasive power of advertising. This is so because advertisers count on our being insecure and fearful regarding our self-image and identity. The words and images advertisers use take advantage of these fears and promise more than their products can ever deliver. With a secure faith in Christ and an identity built upon that faith, the temptation to identify the self with things dissipates. In our faith we are turned toward relationships not things, and in that turn we experience the blessedness of simple living.

Pastoral Suggestions

Parishes can help couples adopt a simple lifestyle by drawing attention to the following principles in homilies and adult education:

1. Money is a means to facilitate the end of marriage and family. It is not an end in itself.
2. The purpose of Christian marriage is holiness. How often have we used our economic resources to facilitate our holiness or to assist others in living out their marriage more faithfully?
3. What concrete things can we do in our family to limit the powerful persuasive effects of advertising? How can we remind ourselves and our children that our dignity lies in Christ and not in *material things*?

IV. HOSPITALITY

An especially useful virtue to the Christian life of marriage and family is that of hospitality. This virtue, like communication, can be based upon one's desire to be affected by God in prayer. In prayer we render ourselves available to be touched by God's life-giving love. We can see an example of this availability in the Angel's announcement to Mary that she was to be the Mother of the Savior. Mary's response is characteristic of all those disciples who have come after her, "May it be done to me according to your word" (Lk 1:38). In Mary, there is the deepest of faith and therefore a depth of availability not only to God but also to all who are in need of God's saving ways. We are open to others to the extent that we ourselves have been affected by the love of God and "lived to tell about it."[16] At times we may fear being loved or needed because we are apprehensive about losing the self. We think love will ask too much of us. This apprehension is a residue of original sin. Psychologically and biologically this fear is linked to our survival instincts. If not exaggerated, this can be good. Theologically, however, it might make us too timid to take risks and to stand in solidarity with others when the immediate "payoff" is unclear.

By hospitality we do not mean simply hosting parties and inviting guests into our home, although this can have its place and significance for other persons' well-being as well as for the quality of our own marriages at times. Here, we are referring to a broader presence to our neighbors than sharing occasional fellowship and a meal. This presence is concerned with the genuine physical and spiritual welfare of those we live near and whom we can concretely aid to fulfill needs. Witnessing to Christ through the service and hospitality of being a good neighbor is a powerful form of evangelization in a society which is too often faceless and nameless.

Indeed, reaching out to others simply to affirm their existence in the neighborhood has become in our day and age a remarkable act since so many of us have come to embrace a very private concept of marriage and family life. This vision of marriage as a "private" act does not welcome others into the space we have reserved for ourselves. In fact, others may be seen as threats or ob-

---

[16] Ex 33 :20ff. "But my face you cannot see, for no man sees me and still lives" (*New American Bible*, St. Joseph Edition, 1970). On the issue of Christian hospitality, see also John Koenig, *New Testament Hospitality: Partnership with Strangers as Promise and Mission*, Overtures to Biblical Theology Ser. (Philadelphia: Fortress, 1985); and Parker J. Palmer, *The Company of Strangers: Christians and the Renewal of America's Public Life* (New York: Crossroad, 1992).

stacles to what the married couple perceives as the only real goal of their love: the welfare of one another. Seasoned married couples know this is an unreal and unhealthy concept of marriage. The experience of many years together has taught them that an authentic love inexorably draws them out of themselves and into the larger society. We need to form engaged couples in a broader vision of marriage as *social*: living out of love for and with others. If there is doubt that this is a necessary agenda for marriage formation, just ask those who facilitate marriage preparation programs if they have ever felt that their ministry was perceived by the engaged couples as a roadblock rather than an eagerly anticipated service. The engaged couples' perception that the Church's ministry is a hurdle to jump over in order to get to the real goal of "being left alone together" is indicative of the growing privatization of marriage.

What other attitudes or dispositions might block us from seeing marriage as a means to hospitality? In order to respond best to the presence of others in our lives, we need to cultivate an attitude or stance of availability, of readiness. A readiness to respond, to be open to the presence of others is crucial if we are to rise to a level of excellence in moral living. French philosopher Gabriel Marcel identified some dispositions that will thwart hospitality and thereby inhibit moral growth:[17]

1. Encumbrance: An encumbrance is anything that hinders or impedes one's performance. An outlook on life that reduces persons to what they possess is an encumbrance. The "need" to possess can turn into *being possessed.* Anxieties about health, fortune, power and position can get in the way of our presence to God, ourselves and others. Obsessions about such things can render us *unavailable.*
2. Crispation: Being tied in knots. This second disposition locks us up in a world of self-concern. We become hardened and bent out of shape. We lock ourselves up in our own little

---

[17] Joe McCown, *Availability: Gabriel Marcel and the Phenomenology of Human Openness* (Montana: Scholars Press, 1978).

world and refuse to be open to what is new and/or beyond our control. As a result of this "crispation," we begin to wither psychologically and spiritually. We identify the world with the self and life degenerates into mere existence.[18]

3. Susceptibility: Being highly impressionable and affected by our emotions, we find our self-love only through affirmations from outside ourself. Our life is validated only in the "glances" of others. In effect, then, in our minds we are only what we *think* others *think* about us. The *idea* of the other actually replaces the other and no real intimacy is ever achieved.

4. Moral ego-centricity: This illusionary disposition makes us the center of the universe, reducing other people to obstructions to be removed or circumvented.[19]

All of these are obviously interrelated. They make us unavailable to others. In order to be available we have to know ourselves in the light of God's loving knowledge of us. We need to become as familiar with our *self* as we are familiar with our homes. Only then will we feel free to make both available to visitors. We can only welcome another to what we ourselves inhabit.[20]

In the virtue of hospitality we see clearly the relationship between spirituality and ethics. When we turn devotionally to God and draw our identity from that relationship, the fear associated with being open to others is vanquished. In light of divine love, we no longer fear losing ourself in showing concern for others, but rather we embrace openness to others as a way to find ourself.

Family hospitality involves other virtues, too, virtues such as prudence, courage and charity. Even though we are secure in our love for God and God's love for us, we understand that sin still has power within us and within those whom we welcome into our lives. We understand that those who are selfish can abuse our open

---

[18] McCown 13.
[19] McCown 15.
[20] McCown 19.

generosity. As a result, the capacity for long-suffering is also a pre-requisite for hospitality (the original Latin word *hostia*, "host" in English, meant "victim"). To avoid the suffering which often accompanies hospitality (and here we mean welcoming the presence of others into your lives, not just into your immediate family), some might be tempted to choose *between* family and neighbor. That would certainly ease the tension between openness to family and openness to neighbor, but it would also render one unfaithful to both marriage and hospitality. Instead, it seems that the only morally correct way to enter hospitable living is to do so as a family. Even if only one member of the family is to be available to others and their needs for a certain amount of time, what is crucial is that the decision come from the family in light of its purpose to love each other in God and to love each other for the needs of others. Service to others should never weaken marriage or the family. If it does, that may be a sign that the decision to be hospitable came from somewhere other than the good of the family. The cultivation of a proper formation in the virtue of hospitality will be essential in marriage preparation classes and ongoing adult education, as we wrestle more explicitly with our individualistic and privacy-driven culture in light of the Church's more communitarian vision.

V. SEXUAL ETHICS

Since the close of the Second Vatican Council in 1965, sexual ethics has become the most explosive issue in moral theology. For many pastoral leaders the subject of sexual ethics is dealt with in a perfunctory manner or not at all; pastors would rather not deal with the dissent and controversy which arises out of such teaching and discussion. This is understandable, of course. In the face of so much evidence that so many Catholics have rejected much of the Church's doctrine on sexual ethics, many DRE's and pastoral associates ask, "Why bang your head against a wall?" This leaves us with two unattractive choices: one, yield sexual ethical education to the secular culture, which would delete the faith component of a sexual ethic altogether; or two, continue to teach the rules which are not generally accepted, thus giving the appearance of faith's irrelevance. We think there is a third way, however. This third way revolves around reforming the parish in its spiritual and moral foundations and then re-presenting the sexual ethic from a positive stance highlighting the *truths* within the doctrine and not simply the rules.

To renew the parish morally we need to base our attempts on a renewed appropriation of the Catholic way of life. By saying this, we recognize that the foundations are cracking. During the last thirty years, some positive things have happened in the parish: vernacular liturgy (although reverence and wonder are largely absent); strong lay participation (though they are not always well prepared); the efforts of many clergy to reject clericalism (even as they struggle to articulate a clear priestly identity); the clergy's openness to collaborative ministry (even though they often find it painful to relinquish much that they had come to identify with their role); some progress in developing the parish as a place to form a lay spirituality of home, work, and public life; and a growing respect for an authentic freedom of conscience. Greater attention has to be paid, however, to a genuine *moral* formation in the context of the Church's intellectual, spiritual, and sacramental ethos.

First, the parish is to assist its members to see that moral living has a definite goal: the appropriation of *moral truth* as reflected in the life and teachings of Christ. Leaders within the Catholic parish will want to challenge the *intellects* of parishioners with a doctrine that integrates the sacramental, spiritual, and moral components of the life of faith into a coherent whole. To accept this intellectual challenge is to move people toward satisfying one of our deepest desires: to know the One who is Truth Incarnate and to love that One in the beauty of that truth.

Second, many parishioners discern right and wrong behavior without engaging official Catholic *moral* and *spiritual* formational sources such as the documents of Vatican II, the papal encyclicals, the new *Catechism,* the statements of the National Conference of Bishops, and the lives of the saints. Instead, they have picked up much of what they know from the liturgy, personal and public devotions, and popular secular sources. Some of the moral teachings of the Church are so counter-cultural (e.g., love of enemies, marriage until death, etc.) that they make sense only from within a Catholic ethos. This does not mean that Catholic moral teaching has left the realm of public discourse; it simply acknowledges that the authorities that have formed American sensibilities are distinct from the authority which forms Catholic sensibilities, namely, being claimed by Christ in baptism. For believers, moral truths are seen more clearly from under the water of baptism.

Finally, the desire to know Christ, who is the Truth, is directed and further specified through *sacramental* living. The truths of moral living will be appropriated only, and insofar as, parishioners allow themselves to be claimed by their baptismal and eucharistic identities. The moral renewal of the parish will begin and culminate in the satisfaction of the desire to become one with Christ in moral goodness. This is what Pope John Paul II has taught so often under the theme of re-evangelization. We must have a desire to love Christ, and this desire will be satisfied as we turn to him within the parish — intellectually, spiritually, and sacramentally.

In the area of sexual ethics explicitly, the attitude of the catechists will be an essential component for inviting moral conversion. As is true with any instruction, the attitudinal approach the teacher takes toward the content is crucial to its being accepted behaviorally or even engaged for further scrutiny. Many of us who were formed in faith in the 1970's lived through a time where what we knew of theology, doctrine, and Catholic moral teaching was predominantly the *criticism* of it by influential theologians. To accept the ecclesial doctrine on sexual ethics was seldom encouraged because some instructors had closed off discussion about it in light of their own dissent. We do not believe much of this closing was done with malicious intent. At the time it was thought that to disagree with Catholic sexual ethics was simply "self-evident." Caught up in the enthusiasm of post-Vatican II openness, many catechists and theologians simply presented their personal judgments as the new standard of Catholic sexual ethics. Those who sought a fuller doctrinal exploration were merely tolerated as not having "caught up" yet with the Church's new conversation with culture. The Church's dialogue with culture is crucial and needed. However, the cards were stacked against what students brought to that dialogue, since instructors often implied that moral doctrine was a lingering relic and the insights of modern culture offered more relevance.[21] We live in a culture that is well-schooled in questioning authority. Those born around and after 1960 became well-versed in the skills of criticism. One could say that what was handed on to that generation was simply the skills of criticizing tradition,

---

[21] We think the emphasis on cultural sources over and against ecclesial doctrine arose through the re-presentation by catechists of the popular teachings of such moralists as Charles Curran. During the 1960's, Curran, who favors a development in the Church's teaching on artificial contraception and other sexual issues, reacted against what he saw as the legalism present in Catholic moral doctrine by listening to the experience of lay-people and promoting a scripturally-enhanced moral theology. While his dissent from official Church doctrine is clearly stated, he contextualized it within a larger respect for Catholic teaching authority. However, the careful nuances he included within his dissenting opinions were not always so carefully emulated by the catechists who received his ideas through reading or from priest-students of Curran and other moralists of the 1960's.

In contrast, Germain Grisez emphasizes the obedience due the magisterium on the part of the laity regarding issues of sexuality. In this way, however, he seems to mute the personal appropriation necessary for a moral act to be truly one's own. He highlights the themes of infallibility, revealed truths, and definitive judgments in such a manner that some could see legalism and authoritarianism within his moral methodology. "A faithful Catholic is not in a position to think a moral norm currently proposed by the ordinary magisterium is false, unless there exists a superior source (Scripture, a defined doctrine, or [infallible teaching]) which requires this conclusion" [Germain Grisez, *The Way of the Lord Jesus*, vol. 1 (Chicago: Franciscan Press, 1983) 854].

Whereas Curran does not accept as binding the truths within the ecclesial doctrine on many sexual issues (artificial contraception, homosexuality, etc.), Grisez, while acknowledging the truths, seems to emphasize authority. We think it is better to promote the truths within the teachings and highlight the necessary virtue formation needed to enable people to embrace them and live them out. See Grisez, *The Way of the Lord Jesus*; and Charles Curran, *Christian Morality Today* (Indiana: Fides, 1966) 72-76 (This was a seminal text for many pastoral ministers around the time *Humanae Vitae* appeared). For a good overview of a virtue ethic, see Joseph Kotva, "An Appeal for a Christian Virtue Ethic," *Thought* 67 (June, 1992): 158-180.

not tradition. William Kilpatrick makes a similar point when he notes that it is strange to teach morality by focusing on argument and criticism. This method is like teaching American history and simply telling the students about Thomas Jefferson's slaves or Martin Luther King's adulterous liaisons. There is simply *more* to the story.

> "One great precaution," said Plato, "is not to let them [students] taste of arguments while they are young" — the danger being that they would develop a taste for arguments rather than a taste for truth. Young minds, like young puppies, said Plato, would only "pull and tear at arguments." Such a method might keep youngsters entertained but it would certainly not make them virtuous. For Plato it was much more important for young people to learn a love of virtue than to argue about it. The dialogue was for those for whom the love of virtue was already in place.[22]

As the years passed since Vatican II and the promulgation of *Humanae Vitae*, some theologians became angry at the lack of development in moral doctrine. Those of a younger generation (born c. 1960) do not and cannot share in the anger of the older generation. They do not have the same experience of rejecting "old ways" and feeling the disappointment of not living to see one's new viewpoint vindicated in doctrinal development. In fact, many of these younger people are not interested in rejecting "old ways" at all — they are simply looking for a way to understand their Catholic identity. To make unresolved anger toward authority an implicit content within pastoral education is unjust at the most, and at the least shows a real lack of awareness of the needs of today's young people. If these young people are in marriage preparation classes, liturgical experiences, and retreat settings, they are there not primarily

---

[22] William K. Kilpatrick, *Why Johnny Can't Tell Right from Wrong* (New York: Simon & Schuster, 1992) 88-89.

to *reject* anything but to look for help in accepting what is true and good. An awareness of the real catechetical and theological needs of a new generation of Catholics is probably the most crucial component to a formation in Catholic sexual ethics today.[23]

A. Popular Culture and Its Image of Sex

Analysis of popular culture has to be the starting place for all sexual ethical formation today. Certainly, the influence of television and other forms of media looms large in the consciousness of American Catholics. There is hardly a television show, advertising spot, or music video that represents a sexual ethic one could call authentically Catholic in its values. Of course, the content of popular programming is not devoid of values which support a Catholic sexual ethic, but it is easier to identify those situations or images which contradict or poke fun at Catholic values then those which promote and support them. For example, many television shows, print advertisements, and video images appear to promote or are at least neutral toward fornication, gay and lesbian sexual activity, adultery, contraception, abortion, artificial reproduction, and/or surrogate motherhood. We exist in a culture that draws its values about sexuality from political (liberal, conservative), separatist (body as seen separately from spirit),[24] and individualist (privacy and rights language) categories, rather than from holistic (body/spirit) and ecclesial stances. We do not wish to analyze here the influence of media on religious values, as this has been done many times before. We simply want to draw attention to its influence,

---

[23] See Robert Ludwig, *Reconstructing Catholicism for a New Generation* (New York: Crossroad, 1995). See also Paul VI, *Evangelii nuntiandi* (On Evangelization in the Modern World), Apostolic Exhortation (Washington, DC: USCC, 1976) 79. Additional help in preparing young people for marriage may be found in *Partners in Life and Love* by Joseph Giandurco and John Bonnici (New York: Alba House, 1996). Regarding the sacramental aspects of marriage, see *What God Has Joined* by Msgr. Peter Elliott (New York: Alba House, 1990).

[24] William E. May, *Sex, Marriage and Chastity* (Chicago: Franciscan, 1981) 3ff. Also Gerard Coleman, S.S., *Human Sexuality* (New York: Alba House, 1992).

and state that any educational methodology must have popular culture as its conversation partner in order for Church doctrine to impact the consciences of young adult Catholics.[25]

B. How to Approach Pastoral Formation in the Truths of Catholic Sexual Ethics

First, those doing catechesis should emphasize the human person understood as *embodied*. The Catholic sexual ethic is positive and draws from a vision of the human person that encompasses the body, the soul and the mind. It views the person as responsible and related both to the self and to others in the context of an embodied life before God. The Catholic vision is not reductionist, and resists equating sex to any one element of its meaning. Sexual love is not just for expressing affection, and yet it recognizes and celebrates the emotional depth experienced through sexual intercourse. Sexual expression is not simply a celebration of marital commitment, but is also, if children are conceived, an act that takes the couple beyond their own love to share in the *creative* love of God. In a culture that reduces sexual intercourse to either a simple bodily expression or the activity of emotional release and celebration, the realistic, holistic complexity of the Catholic sexual ethic is an attractive alternative.

This holistic vision of sex carries responsibilities which, when viewed from within a separatist ethic, can appear too burdensome or without merit. A separatist ethic holds that the most vital as-

---

[25] See the following studies on popular culture: Reynolds R. Ekstrom, ed., *Pop Culture, Access Guides to Youth Ministry* (New Rochelle, NY: Don Bosco Multimedia, Salesian Society, Inc., 1989); Andrew M. Greeley, *God in Popular Culture* (Chicago, IL: The Thomas More Press, 1988); Hilary Regan and Alan J. Torrance, eds., *Christ and Context: The Confrontation Between Gospel and Culture* (Edinburgh, Scotland: T&T Clark, Inc., 1992); John Roberto, *Media, Faith, and Families: A Parish Ministry Guide*, Catholic Family Series (New Rochelle, NY: Don Bosco Multimedia, Salesian Society, Inc., 1992); Philip J. Rossi and Paul A. Soukup, eds., *Mass Media and the Moral Imagination*, Communication, Culture, and Theology (Kansas City, MO: Sheed & Ward, 1994).

pect of sexual behavior to consider is the person's motive. This is usually expressed in terms of "Do you love him?" If so, the sexual act appears good. What also must be asked is what this motivation means when expressed through the *body* and *who* it is creating and affecting in this expression. We are not going to gloss over the crisis that confronts pastoral leadership today regarding contraception and the other issues listed above, but it seems best to focus on the spiritual factors that may aid the believer in appropriating Catholic sexual ethics as if they were approaching its truths for the first time. It also appears to us that unless there is to be a development of doctrine regarding any number of issues in sexual ethics, these controversial areas should be placed within a pastoral formation plan that fosters spiritual and moral conversion. What is needed in this area is the insight to see the truths of Catholic sexual ethics. Some of these truths are: the necessity for lifelong commitment as the only worthy environment for sexual expression; the intrinsic moral link within sex between reproduction and lifelong love; and the dignity of both female and male, and, because of this, the necessary affection, respect, and care owed to one's spouse. Those interested in promoting the present Church doctrine cannot just have yet another study group on the documents on birth control, artificial reproduction, homosexuality and so on. Reception of ecclesial doctrine by Catholics is best understood in the context of spiritual conversion toward the love of God, coextensive with moral conversion toward the love of the Good. In other words, even though many Catholics continue to disagree with much of the moral teaching of the Church, the pastoral leader cannot coerce or dominate parishioners, but instead must speak truth, abide with parishioners, pray, and resist the temptation to "speed up" conversions by laying down the law. "The truth cannot impose itself except by virtue of its own truth as it makes its entrance into the mind at once quietly and with power."[26]

---

[26] *Dignitatis Humanae* (Declaration on Religious Freedom) 1. *Vatican Council II: The Conciliar and Post Conciliar Documents*, ed. Austin Flannery, rev. ed. (Collegeville, MN: Liturgical Press, 1992).

On the hierarchy's part there must be funding and serious planning for these spiritual formation processes. In addition, renewed attempts to discover and articulate a more precise language through which to express the truths of Catholic sexual ethics, a language that can open hardened hearts and find pathways to reconciliation, must be considered. For example, it appears counter-intuitive to continue to express the truth about sex being both an act celebrating marital love and union, and one which aims toward procreation in the language of "each and every act must be open to the transmission of life."[27] The human fertility cycle renders this statement meaningless. Couples practicing Natural Family Planning are not engaging in sexual activity which is "open" to procreation during those times of the fertility cycle when it is impossible to conceive. Certainly they are not acting against procreation either, as do those who use artificial contraception as their usual means of spacing births. However, the language is ambiguous: how is a couple "open" to procreation when they knowingly and willingly choose to have sexual relations only during infertile days? The unitive meaning of sex is present, but biological facts tell us that the procreative end is not possible, and yet it is licit to have sex. The unitive and the procreative are not simultaneously constant. We have to do a better job of articulating just what is wrong with

---

[27] *Catechism of the Catholic Church* (Vatican City: Libreria Editrice Vaticana, 1994) 2366. See also Anne E. Patrick, *Liberating Conscience: Feminist Explorations in Catholic Moral Theology* (New York: Continuum, 1996): "I have some sympathy for the traditionalist inclination to hold the line on classical moral norms about sex. Despite serious limitations, these limitations do prevent much harm. However, these norms are not widely observed, their intellectual underpinnings are inadequate, and the absoluteness and rigidity with which they have been communicated are themselves factors that contribute to addictive and oppressive patterns of sexual conduct" (p. 70). See also John Paul II, *Veritatis Splendor* (The Splendor of Truth) (Vatican City: Libreria Editrice Vaticana, 1994) 53.

acting against procreative powers if people are ever to be persuaded of the objective immorality of doing so.[28] The moral problem is not that people have sex when reproduction is impossible. The problem is that persons act sexually in ways contradictory to the fertility of intercourse. Identifying what is immoral about acting against reproductive potentiality is the crux of the matter.

The trouble is that not many people see contraception as an act "against" anything; they only see it as an act for something. It is an act for responsible family planning. The act of contraceptive intercourse is in fact not seen as an act at all; it is simply subsumed under sexual intercourse as an incidental or accidental element. Analogically, to make a fuss over the actual use of contraception to sterilize sexual intercourse is like being upset that one has chosen to wear a blue outfit rather than a red one. The point is the person is clothed, is she not? All that people recognize today, regarding the ethical nature of intercourse, is the question of responsibility. Is it consensual sex? Is it safe sex? The reproductive nature of sex is a secondary consideration and is only to be discussed if one was "irresponsible," namely became pregnant or contracted a disease.

The catechetical challenge is to retrieve the reproductive meaning of sexuality within marriage. This is a challenge because the culture has successfully marginalized the reproductive mean-

---

[28] Benedict Ashley and Kevin O'Rourke, *Health Care Ethics: A Theological Analysis*, 3rd ed. (St. Louis: Catholic Health Association, 1989): "In what sense is a marital act deliberately placed in the infertile period still 'open to the transmission of life'? Certainly this act is not directly or proximately ordered to procreation (since it is sterile). Thus the order is only indirect and remote. This remote ordination, however, does not seem merely to be the circumstantial intention of the agents, but objective and intrinsic to the moral object. It consists in the fact that God through nature has provided that human reproduction should normally result not from single acts of intercourse, but from a permanent partnership bound together by frequent sexual acts, only some of which are directly and approximately fertile. The infertile acts, therefore, are naturally ordered to fertility, although only indirectly and remotely. In this sense, and only in this sense, can they be said to be open to the transmission of life" (p. 265).

ing of sex. However, in its almost obsessive efforts to marginalize reproduction the culture simply points to its centrality even more.

VI. CONCLUSION: IS CATHOLIC MORALITY AN IMPOSSIBLE IDEAL?

In *Veritatis Splendor*, John Paul II writes:

> It would be a very serious error to conclude… that the Church's teaching is essentially only an ideal which must then be adapted, proportioned, graduated to the so-called concrete possibilities of man…. But what are the concrete possibilities of man? And of which man are we speaking? Of man dominated by lust or of man redeemed by Christ? This is what is at stake: the reality of Christ's redemption…. And if redeemed man still sins, this is not due to an imperfection of Christ's redemptive act, but to man's will to not avail himself of the grace which flows from the act.[29]

This is an extremely incisive theological statement which teaches that humans can be good under the power of God by sharing in his life through grace. Is it possible to live a life of chastity before and after marriage? Is cooperation with the full meaning of the unitive and procreative ends of sexual love within reason for married couples? Can the homosexual remain chaste? Can the infertile couple utilize only those means that assist their natural procreative abilities and refuse to engage in those which *replace* these abilities? In answering "yes" to these questions, one is asserting that these activities are the *right* way to behave. The key is to put the possibility of living in these ways in the category of conversion and not obedience to law. In this way the person is encouraged in free-

---

[29] *Veritatis Splendor* 64 & 103.

dom to appropriate the truth of the doctrines over a period of time. In other words, due to the secular and materialist leanings of the present Western culture, people need to live into the truths of Catholic morality over time. We are not to assume that any set period of time for conversion is sufficient or deigned to be *enough* by pastoral leaders. What we need to do is simply abide with people in compassion and explore the truths within the Catholic sexual ethic from many different approaches: personal, biological, psychological, cultural, spiritual, and normative.

What we have found helpful is to avoid rushing the parishioner into closure either for or against Church doctrine. The pastoral minister operates out of trust in the Spirit, a Holy Spirit wanting the salvation of people. Minister out of that trust and then relax. Present the teaching and abide with the person in fidelity to the truth and in light of the circumstances of the parishioner's life. The goal is clear: eventual acceptance of the moral truths found within Church doctrine. What is new today is that this goal is not supported by a similar ethic found within secular American culture. It is this new cultural situation which warrants an *explicit* moral formation in the parish.

Only in a proper marriage formation period and in continuing education after marriage can Catholic couples hope to appropriate the moral truths that the Church presents as necessary for a life of holiness. The virtues of prayer, honest communication, hospitality, temperance in consuming goods, and chastity are all dispositions which can be acquired and are not simply "ideals" in the abstract. However, the present cultural milieu works against finding ready support in the living out of these virtues. Hence, the parish becomes crucial as that gathering of believers where moral support, prayer, and educational resources exist as food for the journey toward goodness.

Chapter Five

SOCIAL ETHICS: THE PUBLIC FACE
OF CATHOLICISM

In this chapter we will explore some of the issues which confront
Catholics in the public forum. The key question is: How can
Catholics be true to the moral impulses of their faith and also remain fully engaged in our pluralistic society? There are distinctive
Catholic positions on issues in social ethics which other citizens
can appreciate and even act upon as their own (i.e., the Church's
position on issues such as war, capital punishment, and race relations). We see that the reasonable deliberations of Catholic social
teaching are founded upon and open to the God who is Truth and
who guides our minds to the Truth. Nonetheless, the Catholic tradition trusts in a faith-imbued *reason* that can find common points
of agreement with those who reason without faith. When the Truth
is discerned it is *of God* no matter whether the one discerning it
has faith or lacks it.

PRELUDE: AN APPRECIATION OF RELIGIOUS LIBERTY

In order to engage in a dialogue about social ethics in a plu-
ralist culture, it is important to respect and promote a most basic
right in public life: religious liberty. This right stands at the center
of the Church's understanding of human rights.[1] Religious liberty

---

[1] John Paul II, *Centesimus Annus* (On the Hundredth Anniversary of *Rerum Novarum*)
(Washington, DC: United States Catholic Conference, 1991) 47.

is based on the dignity of the human person and upon the individual's need to seek the Truth freely. In this search the state must not impede persons from recognizing and celebrating their belief in God through public worship and the promotion of moral teachings. This ability to practice a religion freely within society without undue government restriction is a key to a peaceful, ordered, and moral society. In other words, the Catholic Church believes that without respect for religious freedom persons cannot be ordered to Truth, and therefore cannot be ordered to God. Without religious liberty, many social questions that confront us can only be reduced to political and/or ethical categories, thus denying the involvement of religious convictions in social change. Persons are directed toward freely knowing the Truth in relation to God, and since we are social beings this pursuit is to be protected and even encouraged by government.[2]

The right to religious freedom affords persons the necessary liberty to form and to follow their conscience. Without this right, citizens would be open to coercion from more powerful institutions pressuring them to suppress — or, under threat, even deny — that which is the very source of their convictions: their love of God and the Truths which flow from this love. This would be akin to saying that someone cannot act upon convictions that flow from love of spouse. For instance, it is illogical to ask a husband not to consider his love for his wife, and all her consequent needs and concerns, in a career move to a new state. To deny the influence of his love for her and hers for him would force the husband to judge and decide his behavior upon an illusion. And so it is with our love for God. To act "as if" God is not a factor in our behavioral choices is to deny reality in light of one's identity in baptism. Now, of course, not all behaviors that flow from love of God or spouse are appropriate for public display or even necessarily ordered

---

[2] *Dignitatis Humanae* (Declaration on Religious Freedom) 6. *Vatican Council II: The Conciliar and Post Conciliar Documents*, ed. Austin Flannery (Wilmington: Scholarly Resources, 1975).

toward the public. However, love has effects that have public ramifications.[3] For example, the public behavior of one who has been
formed by devotedly attending to Scripture could be action that
promotes justice and hospitality toward strangers.[4] The devotion
is private, but it leads to public witness out of one's convictions.

The Catholic presence in the world is fueled by such loving
attention to Scripture and to the living presence of Christ within
the mind's search for Truth. The more we center on Christ in worship, piety, and service, the more we become conformed to his mind
and thus begin to think and act like Christ. Thinking with the mind
of Christ sooner or later affects our public behavior. The parable
of the sheep and the goats in Matthew 25 is a good image of what
happens to people who so love Jesus Christ: They begin to treat
people in the same way Christ does and thus are united with them
and him. These disciples give water to the thirsty, visit prisoners,
and the like, and thus are "known" to be disciples of Christ because they are like him in behavior. As Paul Wadell says,

> To love God in charity is to become like God in good-
> ness…. [T]o love is to become like the one we love….
> To be of one heart and soul with God is to be a friend
> of God, to love what God loves, to cherish what God
> values, to want nothing more than whatever God wills.[5]

To love God is to become like God in our public behavior.
What we love forms us in virtue, and our virtue directs our actions.
And in doing these actions which flow from our character, our vir-
tues are in turn confirmed and strengthened.[6] These actions can

---

[3] Michael Himes and Kenneth Himes, *Fullness of Faith: The Public Significance of Theology* (New York: Paulist Press, 1993) 1-27.

[4] Synod of Bishops, *Justice in the World* (Washington, DC: USCC, 1972).

[5] Paul Wadell, *The Primacy of Love: An Introduction to the Ethics of Thomas Aquinas* (New York: Paulist Press, 1992) 75.

[6] Joseph Kotva, *The Christian Case for Virtue Ethics* (Washington, DC: Georgetown University Press, 1996) 105.

be as diverse as the virtues themselves: hospitality, justice, charity, prudence. The fruits of these virtues are then seen in activities which promote, for example, racial harmony, just treatment of prisoners, compassionate care for the sick, and so on. In this chapter we will explore a number of social issues in light of how we, who have been formed in the mind of Christ, might respond to them.

We will limit our reflections to three issues. The first is the identity of the Catholic in public: on the job, in education, in politics, etc. The second is the issue of physician-assisted suicide; and the third is the issue of poverty. Out of all the social issues one could choose to meditate upon, we choose these three because these issues define how faith in God can concretely influence culture. It is necessary for Catholics to drop the mask of the secularist and boldly live as public Catholics, for one's own sake and for the sake of the moral strength of the culture. Building on the strength of a Catholic identity, the members of the parish can then turn in fortitude to society's weakest and most vulnerable, the poor and the ill. If we build up our Catholic character so that we can be courageous in living it out, we will find a voice to speak with and for the poor and ill. In this way the parish renews not only its own moral identity, but also contributes to the moral regeneration of culture. Obviously, the social issues we have chosen to reflect upon do not exhaust the social doctrine of the Church. They do, however, highlight issues which parishioners clearly need to attend to in their Catholic commitment to culture and family, politics, health, and economic justice.

I. THE NEED FOR PUBLIC CATHOLICS: THE ROLE OF FAITH IN SOCIETY AND POLITICS

Just like a married couple, parish members can be tempted to see the mission of their parish primarily as one of "maintaining the house." There is a tension between maintaining the essentials of an institution and furthering the mission that the institution exists to serve.[7] The tension between maintenance and mission cannot be relaxed in favor of either one or the other. If the man and woman who are married gaze only upon one another, their loving and living becomes sterile. Similarly, in the parish if we are only concerned about intra-ecclesial matters, such as who is going to run the bake sale, serve as lector at Mass, and maintain the altar, the mission side of our baptismal identities will wither.

No doubt, intra-ecclesial ministers are vital for the parish. We need well-trained lectors, catechists, and Eucharistic and hospitality ministers. However, while it is recognized that many dioceses have well-run and highly professional training for intra-ecclesial ministries, very few have formation offices that facilitate the lay presence in the world of work, politics, health care, education, and labor. The presence of Catholics in the world who are witnessing to the truths of Catholic moral teaching is essential for evangelization and re-evangelization. The language needed for intra-ecclesial ministry is well developed, but the language needed to articulate the Catholic mission to society is spoken haltingly and without confidence. What do Catholic politicians, for example, need from the parish to function as Catholics within their daily legislative activities? How do nurses live out their baptismal identity on the hospital floor? What does it mean to be a Catholic and a citizen, a Catholic and a professional? These are the questions that await answers, as models are developed for parish life, promoting not only intra-ecclesial ministries for the laity but also lay formation for a Catholic contribution to the secular world.[8]

To highlight this contribution to society by the laity is to emphasize the relationship between being Catholic and the Church's mission of evangelization. A vital source for reflection

---

[7] Karl Ganss and Kathleen Fuller, "Maintenance or Mission," *Today's Parish* 25 (September 1993): 11-12.

[8] See *The Spirituality of Work Series: Business people, Homemakers, Lawyers, Nurses, Teachers, Unemployed Workers* (National Center for the Laity, ACTA Publications, n.d.). See also John E. Linnan, "From Current Crisis Springs Future Parish," *National Catholic Reporter* 32 (May 31, 1996): 6.

upon this relationship is Pope Paul VI's Apostolic Exhortation, *On Evangelization*.[9] While he affirms intra-ecclesial ministries for the laity, he also highlights several key themes within that document which can help elucidate a formation process, enhancing the Catholic presence in the secular world. Four key themes from Pope Paul VI are as follows:

1. Baptism into the Catholic faith is an act of grace that not only identifies the believer as one chosen by God, but, due to this choosing, claims the person for public witnessing in the name of Christ.[10]

2. The goal of this witnessing is to convert "both the personal and collective consciences of people."[11] This witness is to be manifested "silently" through virtuous behavior and "completed" in gaining the ability to explain and justify one's Catholic identity before the secular world.[12] This witness to the world is not to be confused with political or ideological activities, as it always retains a specifically religious finality.[13] In other words, a public Catholic can never be fully faithful to his or her identity if such an identity is reduced to political or ideological motives and formation. The proper source of conscience formation for the Catholic is the social teachings of the Church not political party platforms.[14] The Catholic conscience is primarily but not exclusively formed by attending to social doctrine. The temptation is to align oneself with political parties who agree with ecclesial teaching; but, we must never forget that any party's identity resides in secular

---

[9] Paul VI, *Evangelii nuntiandi* (On Evangelization in the Modern World), Apostolic Exhortation (Washington, DC: USCC, 1976).

[10] *Evangelii nuntiandi* 13, 15.

[11] *Evangelii nuntiandi* 18, 41, 46.

[12] *Evangelii nuntiandi* 22, 28, 30, 44.

[13] *Evangelii nuntiandi* 32, 36.

[14] U.S. Bishops, "USCC Statement on Political Responsibility," *Origins* 25 (November 16, 1995): 382.

philosophies and popular opinion polls and not in the depths of a religious identity.

3. The most appropriate field for the laity to witness to Catholic life is within the secular world, not by further establishing and developing the ecclesial community.[15] The laity are initiated into the Church in order to be Church in the world. This witness is to be accomplished without denigrating or crushing what is secular in the name of the sacred.[16] We are in fact to cherish all that is good and true in the culture, as these areas prepare the way for the world's full acceptance of the Gospel.

4. Being "publicly Catholic" is undergirded and promoted by the Holy Spirit, because it is by the power of the Holy Spirit "in the depths of consciences [that] causes the word of salvation to be accepted and understood."[17]

A. Public Catholicism: A Model for Formation

These key themes from Paul VI give us a framework in which to focus the formation of Catholics within the parish for public witnessing. Clearly, Catholic tradition wishes the lay person to allow the grace of their sacramental initiation to impact the secular character of their daily living. Specific educational forums are needed in the parish wherein professionals, homemakers, and laborers of all sorts can gather and discuss the meaning of their work in light of their Catholic identity. These forums should be balanced between prayer, study, and conversation about real life situations in which people's daily activities engage their Catholic identity either positively or negatively.

It might be best to begin this formation process by inviting all parish members to large plenary sessions so as to address the

---

[15] *Evangelii nuntiandi* 70.

[16] *Evangelii nuntiandi* 55, 20.

[17] *Evangelii nuntiandi* 75.

general issues surrounding public Catholicism. Parishioners could be prepared for this invitation by regular announcements and some mention in homilies. After the plenary sessions, pastoral leadership could encourage common interest groups (such as physicians, laborers, etc.) to meet regularly on their own over the course of a liturgical season. To keep the groups focused, two more plenaries for the whole parish could be planned as a way to support the small groups and continue to link everyone together.

Periodic reassessment is necessary in order to see if the groups have enough resources, are in need of a more professionally-trained pastoral facilitator for a session or two, or simply want to take the group in a direction other than study for awhile (e.g., a spiritual formation or a direct service commitment). It is the experience of those who facilitate catechesis for adults that quite often this learning bears fruit in a deepened desire for prayer or service.

Obviously our goal here is not to recommend a specific model, but to simply encourage formation of parishioners in their public role as Catholics. The goal is to begin a formation process, either humble or elaborate, within which Catholic laity can grow in their awareness and appropriation of their identity as public Catholics.

> [The Church today] is impaired by a separation of the Church and the world, ignoring the religious dimensions of human existence outside the Church, and the worldliness of the Church itself. Not until the lay person, seeking to live with integrity as a Christian and responsibly as a citizen (the Catholic member of the school board, the Catholic executive, etc.) becomes the center of pastoral attention and theoretical reflection will this dichotomy, so self-serving for the Church and so counterproductive for its public mission, be overcome.[18]

---

[18] David O'Brien, *Public Catholicism* (New York: Maryknoll, 1996) 251.

B. Public Catholicism: Sources of Formation

Once the public nature of the Catholic commitment is acknowledged, the role of the social teachings of the Church as content for adult formation becomes clear. The issues that confront society as a whole can seem too large to address within the catechetical and liturgical structures of a parish. However, these issues, such as poverty, capital punishment, physician-assisted suicide, racism, and homosexual rights, all pass through the human heart before they become established either in law or custom. At the heart of social ethics is the question of what each individual believer is attending to in the formation of conscience; as we said above, what we love forms us in virtue, and our virtues direct our actions. And again, this is why Pope Paul VI's emphasis on evangelization of the conscience is so vital. Small group discussion, prayer, reading on one's own or in study groups, and charitable service can all lead to social change — because virtues are thus formed and vices rejected when one pays loving attention to valid sources of Christian formation.

Only after the heart is changed to embrace the good can one move to promote social change through, for example, legislative efforts. Since the key to initiating social change is the conversion of hearts, the individual ought not feel impotent in the face of social issues. Rather, the relationship between social change and personal conversion is one of dynamic relatedness. It is not necessarily a chronological ordering as if upon the moral conversion of one person, or even many, the social structure of racism, or a newfound respect toward the ill or elderly, will automatically follow. There is a mutual relatedness between the social level and personal level of moral change. The social situation works upon the heart, and hearts work to change the social situation, all in the context of one's baptismal identity, cultural forces and legislative initiatives.

The pastoral challenge is to detect if one side or the other is being overemphasized or neglected. If only personal moral conversion is being fostered, awareness of the social level will dimin-

ish. The key to keeping this balance will be to assist in the formation of consciences that always attend to the *public* ramifications
of *personal* choices.

Finally, without a good understanding of a Catholic vision
of the human person, any public conversation regarding what is
right and wrong is in danger of being reduced to one of autonomy,
privacy, and respect for procedure. In other words, much of why
we disagree with one another in this culture on what is right or
wrong is due to our inability to agree on what it means to be a
human being. We end up just getting out of one another's way
(being "non-judgmental"), rather than persuading one another to
love what is good for the human person.

We began this chapter by stating that the flourishing of
Catholic social teaching depends upon the recognition of religious
liberty. This freedom is essential in facilitating citizens' search for
God, who is Truth. Social difficulties arise when freedom is understood simply as a means toward satisfying self-interest. This
incomplete understanding of freedom goes against our transcendent nature — our being created to find completion in God.
George Weigel comments,

> In the opposing corner are those who argue that free-
> dom is constituted by the liberty to pursue one's per-
> sonal gratifications, self-defined, so long as no one else...
> gets hurt. This anorexic conception of freedom is not
> confined... to academe.... [I]t was succinctly formu-
> lated by the U.S. Supreme Court.... "At the heart of
> liberty is the right to define one's own concept of exist-
> ence, of meaning, of the universe, and of the mystery
> of human life." On this understanding of things, de-
> mocracy is merely an ensemble of procedures, largely
> legal.... Democracy has no substantial core... there are
> only the rules of the game.... The gratification of the
> unencumbered, self-constituting, imperial Self is the end

toward which the American democratic experiment is ordered.[19]

The Catholic vision of the human person in society is grounded in our relatedness to one another and God. Our dignity resides in this relatedness, not in some isolating autonomy. In fact, one cannot be free unless one gives the self away in just and loving relationships. The Catholic vision of the human person is summarized well by Kenneth and Michael Himes:

> The immediate experience of communion with God is living in loving communion with one another. Anyone who claims the former without the latter is a liar (1 Jn 4:20). Because God is love, to live in communion with God is to live in loving communion with one another (1 Jn 4:16).... We are more than bearers of rights. Our rights may be respected and yet our true dignity denied. Belonging, respect, friendship, forgiveness, love are essential to human well being, but they are not easily addressed by the language and concept of rights.... Human dignity can be realized and protected only in community.[20]

People are not meant to be alone, because only in relatedness do we come to know our destiny — friendship with God and one another, and ultimately, our sharing in the life of God. The Catholic vision of the human person comes to us today as good news. In a time when many are anxious to control their destiny, and are competing against one another at the expense of relatedness and intimacy, the Catholic vision of the human person affirms our heart's deepest desire: to be oneself in the giving away of that self in the love of God and in service to others.

---

[19] George Weigel, *Soul of the World: Notes on the Future of Public Catholicism* (Grand Rapids: Eerdmans, 1996) 127.

[20] Himes and Himes 163, 169.

To be a public Catholic is to live out of a vision of life and society which holds moral behavior as essential to creating a just society and facilitating intimacy with God. The Catholic is to think and love and act like a Catholic — in public, on the job, in school. But this presumes the proper formation, which is to be centered in the home and assisted by parish education and liturgical resources. The culture is not neutral ground for the working Catholic, but the field upon which to bear witness to the Good and the True in fidelity to one's baptism.[21] Catholics are to approach their work or cultural activities with a sacramental mind set. They are to see the presence of God in the ordinary events of daily life, to treasure that presence, and to stand for that presence when it is diminished through injustice. All of this necessitates an explicit education in conscience so that, again in the words of Paul VI, the laity can be "initiated into the Church in order to be Church in the world."

C. Pastoral Suggestions

1. Culture embraces all socially transmitted behavior patterns, arts, beliefs, institutions and other products of human work and thought characteristic of a specific community or population. It is the public expression of the values and traditions held collectively in any society. These values are articulated through the media, entertainment, education, and religion. What are the sources you really attend to in the formation of your values — radio, television, popular magazines, religion, teachers, spouse, economic realities? Does your faith fit prominently in this formation? Why or why not? How can the parish help you to be faithful to your Catholic faith while on the job, in political decision making, in teaching, etc.? Read Romans 12:1-2: In what ways do you conform to this age;

---

[21] James A. Coriden, *The Parish in Catholic Tradition* (New York: Paulist, 1997) 106.

and in what ways do you dissent? What is good about this age? What is dangerous about it? Would someone who is visiting you at home know you are Catholic? Would someone who is visiting you at work know you are Catholic?

2. What does Colossians 3:1-4 mean to you about your ordinary daily life as a Catholic? In what ways are you a public Catholic? In what ways do you hide your faith? Is it ever prudent to hide the fact that you are a Catholic? Is it ever prudent to remain silent about a Catholic moral teaching (about welcoming different races, sexual ethics, abortion, capital punishment, consumerism, etc.) when it is being criticized or ridiculed in public? Why? Why not?

3. Read 2 Corinthians 6:14-18: What should our relationship to the culture be? Should we in any way remain separate from it? Why or why not?

II. HEALTH CARE ETHICS

The media is filled with stories dealing with such health care issues as artificial reproduction and assisted suicide. We live in a culture that is constantly being challenged to discern the moral ramifications of new medical technology in relation to treatment decisions for those who are sick and dying. How best shall we care for the ill? Should we support a call for assisted suicide in cases involving the terminally ill? Does suffering have any meaning or should we avoid it at all costs?

More so than with any other ethical issue, the parish is poised to be of great assistance in the formation of Christian consciences regarding health care. In times of sickness, basic questions about life's meaning arise. Those baptized into the life, suffering, and death of Christ need to be formed in the vital truths regarding the meaning of suffering and the acceptance of healing or death. In fact, reflection on a Christian health care ethic should be grounded in a vigorous formation in the theology of baptism. In this way an explicit consciousness of what life in Christ means can guide decisions about illness, suffering and death.

Baptism is a person's symbolic and salvific initiation into Christ's life as mediated by the Church. In the baptismal life, one learns to rejoice with Christ, trusting in him above all else and depending upon him in times of pain and suffering. The sacrament leads one into a life of faith in Christ, a sharing in the very heart of the paschal mystery. Therefore, Christians sense that all they live through, even sickness and dying, can be incorporated into Christ's abiding intimacy with them. This ability to connect one's life with a deep trust in Christ's abiding presence is the work of a lifetime of personally appropriating what happened objectively at baptism. The seeds of courage are planted in the heart at baptism and can come to fruition if cared for through pastoral formation. This formation is one that is grounded in the confidence of Romans 8, wherein Paul reminds us that nothing can separate us from the love of God. Experientially, we know that God's love remains, despite appearances to the contrary, in those times of failure, hardship, and loneliness that we somehow come through without losing faith.

Ministers cannot normally come into a dying person's hospital room and there begin to form the heart and the imagination to trust the love of God and live the paschal mystery — *this was to have been the work of a lifetime of faith formation in the parish.* This need for formation does not mean that it is exclusively entrusted to ordained or lay ministers, since certainly most formation in the faith occurs or does not occur in the family. However, it does fall to the pastoral staff of the parish to orchestrate, facilitate, and oversee explicit faith formation, to help families with this important work.

A. Physician-Assisted Suicide

The U.S. Supreme Court has recently decided that there is no constitutional right to assisted suicide. In other words, it was decided that no one is owed access to a physician's services and medicines supplied by him or her that cause one's own death. The court simply judged that we have no constitutional *right*. The door was left open for state legislatures to enact laws allowing physician-assisted suicide, as indeed has happened in the state of Oregon. The fact that a large part of the population has come to the point of accepting physician-assisted suicide as a good is indicative of just how far reverence for the sanctity of each and every human life has declined in the West. The issue is this: Can we promote what is in itself a good — individual self-determination — if that means condoning consent for assisted suicide? Proponents of assisted suicide are asking citizens to take a narrow social understanding of freedom — choice — to its ultimate limit: If I choose to kill myself, it becomes ethically justified because I *chose* it.

Because it recognizes life as a precious gift from God, Catholic moral tradition rejects physician-assisted suicide. To be given the gift of life is not a license to do whatever one pleases with it, because the donor — God — had an intention in giving. At the very least, one can say the Giver's intention is not to have the recipient destroy the gift.

> [A] gift which remains a gift is always something which signals the disposition and character of the giver. If the disposition of the giver becomes lost to view, then what was a gift becomes merely a possession. This is why things we have received as gifts remain important to us, not because we have exclusive rights to their use, or because of their monetary value, but because they signify the love of the one who gave. A gift ceases being a gift to us to the degree to which the dispositions and heart of the giver become unimportant.
>
> Human life is a gift which is meant to teach us about the dispositions of the [G]iver of life. [God] is essentially a giver. He did not and does not retain life within Himself. He would have the "right" to be the only reality but He wished matters otherwise. He is generous and calls us to a like generosity. To understand the gift

quality of human life as an entitlement to unlimited dominion over the gift is to misunderstand the spirit in which it was given. It is to misunderstand the motives of the giver. It is to lose appreciation for life as a gift.[22]

Herein lies our greatest pastoral challenge in all issues of social ethics: the re-establishment of our identities in God. When we center our identities in God's love, we are formed to see that life in any stage or condition is due reverence because the mind perceives that relatedness to God and one another, not radical autonomy, is the key to moral living. Pastorally, there are three things that need to be emphasized in order to assist Catholics and others in society to re-think the drive to legitimize a terminally ill patient's request for suicide:

1. Replace Autonomy with Theonomy

Stanley Hauerwas once noted that the campaign to defend autonomy and self-determination is the American way of describing loneliness. We have pushed religious communities so far away from ourselves in the name of privacy and self-determination that all we have left is the isolated self. The parish can be the place where a cultural revolution begins. It can be a gathering of believers who will not cling to the primacy of privacy, but rather celebrate relatedness as the core of human reality. This kind of parish can become a source of virtue which leads persons to acts of courage in the face of suffering, compassion in the face of a neighbor's sickness, and to prayer in the face of our limitedness. Certainly privacy is a legitimate need for all, particularly in sensitive areas involving the preservation of confidential material. However, even respect for freedom of conscience is contextualized in a communitarian rationale. In order to flourish as a *society*, we need privacy. Privacy unhinged from community interests cannot bear weight

---

[22] James Keating and John Corbett, O.P., "Euthanasia and the Gift of Life," *Linacre Quarterly* 63 (August, 1996): 39.

as *the* ethical norm. The "I," as symbolized in the drive to exalt privacy as *the* right, is only a portion of reality. Reality from a Christian point of view is reflected more fully in a vision that highlights the "I" as completed in relatedness.

Is it simply a coincidence that the same culture which exalts privacy and self-determination in the moral realm has now come to argue for the right of individuals to be killed upon request? Might it not be true that, in our mightily fought victory to be left alone, physician-assisted suicide appears as the *spoils* of such a battle?

The difficult work of forming a parish community in Christ attempts to balance relationships between self, others, and God. In the 1970's, we put a lot of emphasis on the self in every area of culture but worship. There the reverse was true. As we moved from a stress on private prayer and adoration in worship to fuller community participation, a sense of the transcendent was dimmed or lost entirely. Communal participation in worship and in parish decision making was good, in fact essential, and can never be allowed to recede to the background as it apparently did in the days prior to Vatican II. However, the transcendent relationship of God with each and every individual human person remains essential to spiritual growth and salvation. Identifying the self or the community with images that are predominantly political or cultural leads not to the Truth, but to half-truths. No doubt it is difficult to form people in the fullness of their baptismal identity — which includes self, others, and God — but it will be this kind of formation that can mute the excesses of an individualism and secularism born only of political realities. Doing the hard work of forming Catholics in the *fullness* of their human identity can be the concrete parish contribution to halting the drive toward acceptance of physician-assisted suicide, or any exaltation of privacy and autonomy in contradiction to the reality of relatedness. The greatest contribution a parish can make, however, lies not simply in educating parishioners in these truths but in helping people to actually live these truths in society. Forming Catholics who refuse to participate in activity directed *against* innocent life, while supporting activities that *pro-*

mote justice, is one of the clear aims of parish religious education. Walter Kasper has noted:

> Human freedom only arrives at completion and fulfill-
> ment through theonomy (rule by God) — through the
> recognition of God and through fellowship with God.
> For part of human freedom is openness into the infi-
> nite mystery…. So theonomy brings autonomy to ful-
> fillment as autonomy. The greater unity with God, the
> greater the freedom of the human being.[23]

To be disposed to act against the good of innocent human life by partaking in assisted suicide is to know not freedom but enslavement. The self is too small a reference point for ethical decision making. We were made for communion with God, and in this communion we come to know that life is a gift to be received and known more fully in relation to God, not in exaltation of an autonomous self.

2. Provide Explicit Formation in Issues of Death and Dying

The two taboos of western culture remain: sex and death. We saw in Chapter Four how difficult it is for the parish to sustain formation in Catholic sexual ethics, and we have a similar difficulty with the subject of death. Since autonomy rules as the guiding ethical principle of current society, we see a similar ethical standard for both sex and death: Whatever two consenting adults do in the privacy of their own room is said to be acceptable. In our sexual lives this principle certainly seems to rule, and now it seems also to rule in the minds of many lay persons and some physicians as they accept assisted suicide.

If parishes would more frequently sponsor forums, missions, and/or adult education classes on death and dying from a Catholic perspective, we might begin to chip away at the false notion that

---

[23] Walter Kasper, *Theology and Church* (New York: Crossroad, 1989) 50-51.

we control all — even our dying. Because we are uncomfortable with death in general, we like to use euphemisms for assisted suicide such as the one created in the Oregon bill legalizing assisted suicide, "aid-in-dying." However, it is more honest to refer to this act not as dying — that is too passive — but as what it really is, viz. killing. It is complicity in the taking of a human life. If we accept this fact, then we can assess whether this kind of killing is in accord with our Catholic tradition. But calling physician-assisted suicide *dying* is disingenuous. John Paul II finds some hope in the use of euphemisms: He believes that since persons still use them, these persons must have an inkling of a social conscience and are, therefore, potentially open to the moral formation a parish can provide.[24]

One very practical way to begin a formation process would be for pastors and religious educators to call an educational summit where they could meet with the health care professionals in their parish. This coalition could be mobilized to educate the consciences of parishioners in health care ethics and in issues surrounding suffering, dying, and death. The linking up of pastoral and medical personnel can help assure that any formation process will be comprehensive, since all too often pastoral emphasis alone is too abstract, and medical input alone can be too technical.

The coalition could have several facets to its mission. First, parish leadership could invite parishioners who labor in the medical profession to work with them to articulate the relationship between faith and the ethical questions of health care. After that, these health care workers could be invited to catechize the parish. The formation of medical people in the teachings of the Church, and the formation of pastoral leaders in the relevant facts of medical science, would establish the first phase of a *parish-wide* education in medical ethics. This would be a dialogue. In no way are Catholic medical professionals aware of the faith's ethical stance on all

---

[24] John Paul II, *Evangelium Vitae* (The Gospel of Life) (Vatican City: Editrice Libreria Vaticana, 1995) 58.

issues. Likewise, many pastoral leaders are unaware of the necessary medical facts regarding many of these same issues. Topics might include the ethics of physician-assisted suicide, futile treatment, living wills, and so on. The goal is to complement one another's knowledge, and thereby cooperatively to empower all the faithful with the spiritual and intellectual formation needed to respond as informed Catholics in matters of life and death.

After gathering pastors, religious educators, and health care workers, we recommend two reading resources to launch the discussion. The first resource is the U.S. Bishops' recently revised directives on health care ethics, "Ethical and Religious Directives for Catholic Health Care Services."[25] They are easy to read for health care professionals and can serve as a good platform for discussion. Second, Edmund Pellegrino and David Thomasma's *The Christian Virtues in Medical Practice* is particularly useful because it is directed toward health care professionals; it focuses upon the unique Christian dispositions which can deepen the physician's reverence for the patient and his or her own calling.[26] From these discussions, or integrated within them, the group can move toward spiritual development. We envision these forums being at once informational and formational, with the goal being both intellectual and moral conversion.

We are convinced that the formation of the parish in issues of health care ethics depends on the active participation of physicians, nurses, and administrators of Catholic hospitals. We realize that in some local areas this formation is sponsored at the diocesan level or at the hospital itself. However, the linking of this for-

---

[25] U.S. Bishops, *Ethical and Religious Directives for Catholic Health Care Services* (Washington, DC: United States Catholic Conference, 1995). See the excellent commentary on these Directives by Kevin O'Rourke, O.P., and Jean de Blois, C.S.J., "Introducing the Revised Directives: What Do They Mean For Catholic Healthcare?" *Health Progress* 76: 3, 4 and 5 (April, May, and June 1995). See also *Medicine and Christian Morality*, 3rd edition by Thomas J. O'Donnell, S.J. (New York: Alba House, 1996).

[26] Edmund Pellegrino and David Thomasma, *The Christian Virtues in Medical Practice* (Washington, DC: Georgetown University Press, 1996).

mation with one's community of worship is a powerful formative experience that underscores the relationship between ethics and spirituality in everyday living.

3. Move the Sick to the "Sacred Center" of the Parish

Those members of the parish who are ill are usually well attended to by pastoral ministers. Priests and other ministers visit hospitals, nursing homes, hospices, and family residences on a regular basis to maintain the parishioner's connection to the parish during a time of sickness. This is as it should be. However, it appears that the notion of sickness itself, in a culture obsessed with health, well-being, and youthful vitality, is submerged in our consciousness, only to appear when we are battling illness in our own lives. To some extent the sick are "out of sight, out of mind," even as we publicly debate health care insurance and wellness programs. This marginalization of the sick within our consciousness can in part facilitate an acceptance of physician-assisted suicide. Many of us do not know the sick or see the sick. We shield ourselves from them and quite often avoid them in an effort to escape our own mortality. The parish can help us resist the reduction of sick persons to morbid reminders of our own mortality by humanizing sickness and putting a "face" upon it.

It should not surprise anyone that some of the lonely and pain-racked sick want to kill themselves — many chronically ill persons report feeling alienated and useless. One root of evil is isolation and prolonged loneliness. It is not good for us to be alone. Prolonged loneliness is an inherently anti-human condition, and thus a breeding ground for sin. The sick should be at the sacred center of our parishes. They are to be held up in prayer. Communal celebrations of the Anointing of the Sick should be a regular occurrence within the parish. Sincere efforts to visit the sick and attend to their *real* needs should be undertaken. Each parish has to reassess their approach to this ministry in light of their own fiscal and personnel resources. However, in light of the current cultural bias against the sick, this ministry should be a priority and pastoral leaders need to be open to conversion regarding their current use of resources.

B. Pastoral Suggestions

1. Does the parish provide regular forums on sickness, suffering, and dying from a Catholic perspective, not simply a legal forum on living wills or the like?
2. Are the sick regularly prayed for by name? Can we think of creative ways to bring the sick to mind and thus to prayer? Some parishes have discontinued the practice of publicly blessing and dismissing the Eucharistic ministers who take communion to the sick. Pastors should rethink this and perhaps reinstate it where possible, as a powerful reminder of our unity with sick and absent members of the parish. Some parishes occasionally place dignified and appropriate photographs of those who are ill on posters in the vestibule to remind parishioners of specific persons and their prayer needs. This concretizes the sick as real people, with real faces. Celebrating the Anointing of the Sick regularly within the Mass brings the suffering before God and brings the sick before the minds of the praying community.
3. Third, pastors could host a White Mass, a smaller, local version of what many bishops celebrate for health care professionals each year. After the pastor or other qualified person preaches about healing and health care ethics, the parish could host a meal and invite a competent person to facilitate a reflection on what it means to be a Catholic health care professional, then he or she could elicit conversation and questions.

III. POVERTY

As with all social issues, poverty is not solvable within the parameters of the mission of a parish. We can certainly share our wealth in charity with those who are poor, but reducing poverty within our culture is only achieved through the collaborative efforts of government, business, and other mediating structures of society. Nonetheless, the parish certainly has a role to play in the efforts to reduce poverty, through its educational commitments and its primary mission of teaching all that they are loved by God. Believing in their lovability helps the poor by engendering self-respect and encourages the wealthy to be generous in creating employment opportunities and in giving to charitable organizations.

The first explicit role of the Catholic parish in assisting the poor and reducing poverty's reach into families is not primarily directed toward the poor themselves. Rather, it is a sustained effort to educate the faithful, and especially Catholic business and government leaders, in their moral duties relative to the issues of poverty. Simultaneously, parishes can help educate members about the virtues of initiative and creativity, as well as referring economically poor parishioners to organizations that train persons in specific employment skills. Obviously a parish can not "do it all"; but poor parishioners should be able to rely on pastoral ministers to refer them to agencies which can assist them in their very real needs.

A. Rich and Poor Working Together

It is too simplistic to blame all poverty on the greed of the rich. At the same time, as we noted in Chapter Four, it is equally simplistic to deny that wealth can be dangerous to the soul. Riches are a necessary evil, as it were. Without wealth there can be no employment of the poor. Unless we want a state-run economy — and its failure wherever it has been tried should dampen that desire — private wealth is essential as the means of production and employment. Material poverty is an unquestioned evil. If those who are poor are called blessed by Scripture, it is because God has a special predilection for them. He looks with compassion on their openness, trust and dependence upon him. Being poor does not make one holy; being rich does not make one evil. The Catholic tradition insists that both the wealthy and the poor rely upon God, adore God, and worship God so that God can have an effect on their lives. The effect God has on rich and poor alike is concrete, summoning both to real moral conversion and to work for structural change where needed.

Second, Catholicism invites the poor and the rich to join together in a relationship of love for their mutual benefit, a relationship free of all hint of exploitation, envy or disdain. Donal Dorr writes that a spirituality of social concern is one that is both community-minded and character-forming of the individual minister. Such a spirituality challenges us to *go deep* into our converted hearts in order to find strength and a reason to *abide among the poor*. For Dorr, this heart is converted three ways: morally, religiously and politically. The first is a conversion to virtue, the second is a turning toward love, and the third is an awakening to the fact that society is created and not simply "there."[27]

It is through the third conversion that both the rich and the poor come to know one another in community. The building of society is not the work of those persons alone who have societal influence, but is rather the task to which all citizens contribute. Such a joint effort seeks to assure an equitable distribution of power and influence among all elements in society. Thus, the just society educates all, protects all, empowers all to gain work, housing, food and health care and to enjoy productive and fulfilling lifestyles. All — not the few, not the many, but *all* — are to participate in shaping the culture in which they want to live. This universal participation is the ideal towards which we must strive and it acts as a standard that promotes and protects the worth of all citizens. This achievement is the fruit of a spirituality of solidarity with the poor.

---

[27] Donal Dorr, *Spirituality and Justice* (Maryknoll, NY: Orbis Books, 1984) 16.

B. Pastoral Strategies Against Poverty

Poverty is closer to many than they imagine. Many lower and middle-class people are one or two paychecks away from being poor, maybe even homeless. One can be poor as the result of personal vice, but one can also be a victim of market forces or of ethnic, racial, or religious discrimination. Many women and their children are disproportionately poor as a consequence of marital failure. No one has found the key to ending poverty forever ("The poor you will always have with you," Mt 26:11) but some factors do seem to be critical, such as the need to promote personal self-esteem, the importance of acquiring marketable skills and the availability of a job that pays a family wage. Owners of the means of production must refrain from any unjust treatment of their workers, and must practice the virtues of honesty, courage, and creativity so important to ensuring the viability of their business for the good of the community.

Catholics are prominent throughout the marketplace as both employers and employees. Thus the importance of their formation in the area of social justice. Catholic social teachings are rather complex, not because they are arcane but because they are so inclusive. It is hard to reduce any one player in the economy to being the bad guy. The Church's teaching does not simplistically blame the poor for their poverty, nor does it use the rich as scapegoats for society's ills in an effort to divide the classes. Instead, the teachings hold up certain virtues and principles in which *all* Catholics should be formed. The moral goal is to decrease the number of those in poverty by increasing opportunities for participation in the economy.

The production of goods and services is everyone's responsibility, and their fair distribution is owed to every citizen. The economy is to serve the common good. A goal in any economic ethic is to adjust practices and policies in favor of increased participation by all citizens in the economy, which by and large simply means increased employment at a family wage. The pastoral obligation is to do a minimum of two things. First, pastors must decry poverty — shout, draw attention to it as an evil. This is the prophetic heritage. Second, they must act to form parishioners in those virtues that enable them to "see" the marginalized, the unemployed, and the poor. The more we form people in Christ's compassion, hospitality, and service to others, the more parishioners will think out of hearts which incline to the poor. Beyond this, parishes can help form people in the virtues of industry, creativity, and initiative. It may be politically incorrect to raise the issue of indolence and ignorance regarding the plight of the unemployed, but it remains true that in some instances people could improve their economic situation through personal initiative and hard work. Personal failure, however, has to be seen within the context of the individual's personal circumstances. Family breakdown, drugs, poor health, lack of opportunity or encouragement, all exacerbate the problem. Personal vices and cultural forces can entrap one in a vicious cycle of dependency from which it is hard to extricate oneself.

Further, the pastoral agenda to overcome poverty must include two things: direct service to the poor and the formation of virtue. Direct service includes volunteering at food pantries and homeless shelters, building affordable housing, and supporting charities such as the St. Vincent de Paul Society. And we can form the rich and poor in virtue by helping them to overcome at least some of the hardness of heart and blindness to others' needs which compounds the problem of poverty. Simultaneously, pastoral leaders can encourage industry and initiative by involving parishioners in services of charity, worship and attention to examples of sanctity and virtue.

C. Schooled in the Virtues

In no way are these two efforts aimed at denying or denigrating the reality of structural sin, which also plays a part in keeping the poor in poverty. However, most structural sin has personal roots and, therefore, efforts at facilitating personal conversion ought to be a primary mission within the parish. Focus on personal conversion also recognizes the limits of a parish's public role. The power of legislation is needed to keep structural sin in check (e.g., racist practices). After this is accomplished, inculcating the virtues of leadership and citizenry is needed in order to keep sin from becoming entangled in public structures again. In the end, it is the parish which can assist in the formation of people who do not fail to see the poor, take initiative to not be poor (i.e., via education, skills training, etc.), and agitate for change when the law unjustly treats the poor. As the Pope reminded us in a recent visit to the United States: "In America, Christian faith has found expression in an impressive array of witnesses and achievements. We must recall with gratitude the inspiring work of education carried out in countless families, schools and universities, and all the healing and consolation imparted in hospitals and hospices and shelters. We must give thanks for the involvement in political life, in a wide variety of charitable and social organizations, and in the growth of ecumenical and inter-religious understanding and cooperation."[28] Religion shapes the kind of character without which a democracy cannot survive.

In following these formation goals of decrying poverty, forming parishioners in virtue, and agitating for structural change when needed, the parish can add its small but necessary voice to the entire society's efforts to increase people's participation in the economy so that all people may live above the poverty level. The parish can be a powerful force for moral conversion in its forums for education, worship and service. The key to forming parishioners in Catholic social teachings is to base most educational processes upon *local* social analysis. In this analysis, the real situation of parishes is noted and assessed on the economic, familial, spiritual, and health levels. The parish is part of a universal Church and

---

[28] Pope John Paul II, Homily at Mass on Oct. 8, 1995, in Oriole Park at Camden Yards, Baltimore, MD.

this identity should be highlighted; however, frustration levels rise, as do feelings of impotence, when the focus of social ethics formation is disproportionately national or worldwide in scope. No doubt it is important to know about and act upon the needs of those in foreign lands. Conversion of mind and heart, however, needs to be fed by direct service to those locally who are economically deprived as well as to those who are needy in ways that have nothing to do with economic deprivation. Some wealthy suburban parishes may have no economically poor within their boundaries, but are afflicted deeply with poverty of the soul and a lack of intimacy. Cognizant of the many levels of deprivation persons can experience, parishes ought to analyze their local situation and aim ministerial responses accordingly.[29]

> Social analysis says my love is serious enough to want to discern, "What is really helpful in this situation?" Social analysis is an instrument for standing with the poor… which clears our thinking to judge differently what we see. Social analysis helps the Church do its job better, which is the preaching of the Gospel…. Social analysis enables [ministers] to avoid being merely good agents of socialization [and to] ask, "What really is going on here?" from various vantage points.[30]

To respond to the needs of the poor, the parish has to be schooled in the virtue of seeing or contemplating,[31] as well as in the discipline of self-forgetfulness. If we continue to fear that our own needs will not be met, those who truly lack material and spiritual resources will languish — partly as a result of the rich's in-

---

[29] Three good resources to help organize a parish's response to the need for formation in Catholic social ethics are: U.S. Bishops, *Communities of Salt and Light: Reflections on the Social Mission of the Parish* (Washington, DC: USCC, 1994); *Communities of Salt and Light: Parish Resource Manual* (Washington, DC: USCC, 1994); and Fred Kammer, S.J., *Salted With Fire* (New York: Paulist, 1995) 38-68.

[30] Kammer 42-44.

[31] *Evangelium Vitae* 83.

ability to trust that enough possessions are enough. We should be trusting that God will see to *our* needs and in that trust turn to respond to the needs of others. Those who forget self will themselves find in that very forgetting a fidelity to their human identity.

D. Pastoral Suggestions

1. Have the diocese sponsor a retreat for Catholic political leaders in the local area, to reflect on and pray over the implications of Catholic social teachings, in relation to the leaders' respective positions as lawmakers, judges, mayors, council persons, etc. If there are several political leaders in your own parish, you may want to sponsor a smaller gathering either at the parish itself or at a local retreat house. The key focus of the retreat would be to introduce the political leaders to the principles of Catholic social teaching and then to have them identify where those teachings can assist them in the day-to-day questions of their office. Share what virtues they need in order to approach their work with a proper disposition. It might also be an appropriate time for the leaders to articulate how allegiance to a political party can be balanced with allegiance to religion, family, and nation.

It may be difficult for this suggestion to come to fruition, because some Catholic politicians fear that participating in such a retreat will be perceived as violating the principle of separation of Church and State. However, educating oneself, out of one's own resources, how one's profession relates to one's faith is hardly a violation of that principle. The other fear of politicians will be that Father or some other ecclesial minister will tell them how to vote. This fear can be alleviated by focusing the retreat not on *issues*, but on what *sources* form a Catholic conscience and character. If the politician rejects this, to whom or to what sources does he or she go to have character formed specifically as a Catholic?

2. Begin each parish meeting by asking, "How is what we are about to do here going to affect the poor and sick of our parish?" This would help to raise awareness of how receptive the structures of the parish are to the poor.

3. Can it go without saying that the parish administration, as employers, must be just in the wages they pay to employees?[32] There is a continued discussion over the relationship between recognizing the fiscal constraints of some parishes and the need to pay just salaries to professionally trained pastoral ministers. Of course, one may always give freely to the parish out of love; however, this should never be inferred as an expectation for professionals. The need to pay just salaries to parish employees is not simply the pastor's responsibility — the congregation should be concerned that their fellow Catholics are being paid sufficient wages at their own parish, and act in ways to increase those wages according to the local situation. Frank Almade notes:

Pastors know that most parishes are only supported by 30-40% of hard-core regular contributors. These observations indicate ability to contribute. The money is there. The number of untapped potential donors is large. American Catholics... have funds to contribute to the continued ministry of the Church through paid workers given a just wage. The common good calls for those parishes with greater sources of donated income to share with the poorer parishes.[33]

---

[32] U.S. Bishops, *Economic Justice for All* (Washington, DC: USCC, 1986) 351. See also Coriden 112ff.

[33] Frank Almade, *Just Wages for Church Employees* (New York: Peter Lang, 1993) 143. See also Patrick McNamara and Charles Zech, "Lagging Stewards," *America* 175 (9/14/96): 9-14.

IV. CONCLUSION

In this chapter we wanted to highlight the interpenetration between the formation of personal virtue in the parish, and its effect in shaping public life and issues. There is an identifiable Catholic stance toward work, professional health care issues, and economic policy, as well as an array of other social issues. The parish and its explicit formation processes stand in the breach between the individual and the individual's contribution to the moral progress of society. The effort needed by pastoral leaders to bring parishioners to an awareness of Catholic social teaching is usually greater than the effort needed to educate on personal moral issues. The key to alleviating any resistance to this kind of education is to clearly connect the personal to the social. The connection between the distinct levels of personal experience and the urgency of social issues can be made through our identities as persons in community and as communities of persons. The parish is a pivotal participant in the process of forming parishioners as public Catholics. By the continuing education of adults in various pastoral forums, preparation for the evangelization of society can continue.

CHAPTER SIX

MORAL FORMATION IN THE PARISH

We have examined specific areas in which parishes will influence the public witness that Catholics can give to society. The parish staff's primary task is to create a community formed by the Gospels and inspired by the Church's teachings. These communities should be supportive, caring places in which people are formed to go forth and witness to the Kingdom in their everyday lives. In this final chapter we will discuss five areas of parish life that can foster this formation: preaching, evangelization, the small group experience, nurturing our youth, and the sacrament of reconciliation.

I. PREACHING

The pulpit is the one place where preachers can reach the greatest number of people in the shortest space of time. It is a well-known fact that most Catholics value and crave good preaching. For a variety of historical reasons, good preaching was not always a high priority among Catholics. This is no longer the case. When we join the desire for good preaching with the transmission of the Church's moral tradition, we have the ingredients for prophetic preaching.

In discussing the prophetic dimension of preaching, we presume that the basic principles for good preaching and the time needed to prepare good homilies are high on the priority list of any preacher. Although preaching within the Eucharistic liturgy is generally limited to ordained ministers, there are times and places where the laity can legitimately preach, e.g., prayer services, Liturgy of the Hours, communion services, retreats, etc. In addition, we suggest that preaching be looked at not only in the narrow sense of the liturgy and prayer services but also in the broader sense of the teaching of the message that goes on in the classroom and religious education centers. What preaching and teaching share in common is the goal of raising peoples' consciousness about the meaning of Christian faith. In this sense, every homily is teaching and every good teacher is preaching. Thus, both preachers and teachers in parish programs share in the prophetic mission of the Church.

A. Prophetic Preaching

When bringing the moral teachings of the Church into our preaching, we need to give serious consideration to the prophetic call. This is no easy task. As Winston Churchill once said, "I always avoid prophesying beforehand, because it is a much better policy to do so after the event has already taken place."[1] It is usually hard to preach about issues that are unresolved and about which people have strong feelings. For example, the vast majority of Americans, including Catholics, favor the death penalty. We need to proclaim the Gospel message of life even when we know that it might be met with resistance and even hostility.

Tradition and contemporary experience teach us that often pain, rejection, and sometimes death is a prophet's fate. Churchill was indeed right when he said that it is easier and more socially acceptable to speak the prophetic word after the event has occurred. The problem is that the delayed message can no longer be called prophecy. The Church's preaching should include a prophetic

---

[1] Sir Winston Churchill, Press Conference, Cairo, February 1, 1943.

component. All too often, we react after the fact rather than responding to and challenging religious, political, and social events that are contrary to the values of the Gospel. If we fail to communicate to the Christian community the challenges of the Gospel and the teachings of the Church then we become part of the problem rather than part of the solution.

In the Hebrew Scriptures, the prophets spoke to a particular political and religious environment. They were attuned to the issues and concerns of their day. Those who had an especially profound impact on Israel's religion are referred to as classical prophets. Walter Brueggemann writes that these people were often responsible for an alternative community to the existing power structures.

> The task of the prophetic ministry is to nurture, nourish, and evoke a consciousness and perception alternative to the consciousness and perception of the dominant culture around us.[2]

The heart of the prophetic mission lies in the ability to criticize and energize. What Brueggemann means by this is that the prophet is called to challenge institutions by pointing out their shortcomings. But it would be a mistake to stop there. That would not make one a prophet. There are too many people today who are obsessed with talking about what is wrong with contemporary society. The true prophet is one who can move beyond that and energize a community to re-image, renew, and rebuild. That is the prophet's ultimate goal.

It is important to note that the prophets never proposed programs of social action. They did not use their preaching forum to give seminars on the politics of their day. Rather, they spoke about their experience of God and gave people clear principles from which to operate.

---

[2] Walter Brueggemann, *The Prophetic Imagination* (New York: Fortress Press, 1978) 13.

There were two characteristics of the prophets that made them effective preachers. First and foremost they were people of conviction. Maybe Jeremiah, because of his deep sensitivity, is the best example of this depth of feeling:

> My anguish, my anguish!
>   I writhe in pain!
> My heart is beating wildly;
>   I cannot keep silent;
> for I hear the sound of the trumpet,
>   the alarm of war.
> Disaster overtakes disaster,
>   the whole land is laid in waste.
> Suddenly my tents are destroyed,
>   my curtains in a moment.
> How long must I see the standard,
>   and hear the sound of the trumpet?   (Jr 4:19-21)

Jeremiah exhibited a sensitivity that so many around him had lost, especially the kings and priests. It was precisely his deep feeling and awareness that enabled him to penetrate the issues of his day and begin to move the community to new insights. His poetic insight indeed was transformed into a prophetic message.

The prophets were also able to call people to a new hope. To leave people in the depths of despair over their sins and mistakes would be self-defeating. Second Isaiah did this for his people. He brought a comfort that gave them the security to move forward:

> Comfort, comfort my people, says your God.
> Speak tenderly to Jerusalem,
> and proclaim to her
> that her service is at an end,
> her guilt is expiated.   (Is 40:1-2)

While Israel found herself in the depths of despair, the prophet kept calling her to new heights. It was the energy of this hope that gave Israel the courage to create new beginnings:

Get up onto a high mountain,
Zion, herald of glad tidings;
Cry out at the top of your voice,
Jerusalem, herald of good news!
Fear not to cry out
and say to the cities of Judah:
Here is your God!
Here comes with power
the Lord God,
who rules by his strong arm. (Is 40:9-10)

Among the models of the Church proposed by Avery Dulles is the "Church as Herald."[3] Christ commissioned the community to "Go forth and make disciples of all nations.... Teach them to carry out everything I have commanded you" (Mt 28:19-20). The preacher's role is to assist the Church in carrying out this mission. Richard McBrien clearly articulates this task:

> The mission of the Church is one of proclamation of the Word of God to the whole world. The Church cannot hold itself responsible for the failure of men to accept it as God's word. It has only to proclaim it with integrity and persistence. All else is secondary. The Church is essentially a kerygmatic community which holds aloft, through the preached word, the wonderful deeds of God in past history, particularly his mighty acts in Jesus Christ. The community happens wherever the Spirit breathes, wherever the Word is proclaimed and accepted in faith. The Church is event, a point of encounter with God.[4]

The role of the preacher is to enliven the faith of the community and to challenge it to speak and live Christ's message fearlessly in the marketplace.

---

[3] Avery Dulles, *Models of the Church* (New York: Image Books, 1978) 76-89.

[4] Richard McBrien, *The Church: The Continuing Quest* (New York: Newman Press, 1970) 11.

All preachers must search their hearts as to whether their lives and words are being faithful to the Gospel and responsible to the communities where they preach. Karl Barth warns of the tendency among preachers to domesticate God's Word. Softening the message is to do violence to God's Word and to cheat the community of what is rightfully theirs. For example, preachers take away the radical call to Christian forgiveness when they say things like: "In today's aggressive world we cannot live this way. Besides, Jesus didn't mean for us to take his teaching on forgiveness literally."

The American bishops echo this same concern in their document about preaching, *Fulfilled in Your Hearing*.[5] They write, "The preacher represents this community by voicing its concerns, by naming its demons, and thus enabling it to gain some understanding and control of the evil which afflicts it."[6]

The bishops at the Second Vatican Council in the Dogmatic Constitution on Divine Revelation presented a dynamic understanding of God's revelation. From this vantage point, preachers must listen to God's Word and interpret it for the community. In doing this, the Church must call the community to respond to the issues that confront today's society. After all, how can we claim to follow Christ if we do not respond to the people's needs? The Council was very clear about this point:

> The joy and hope, the grief and anguish of the men of our time, especially those who are poor or afflicted in any way, are the joy and hope, the grief and anguish of the followers of Christ as well. Nothing that is genuinely human fails to find an echo in their hearts. Christians cherish a feeling of deep solidarity with the human race and its history.[7]

---

[5] National Conference of Catholic Bishops, *Fulfilled in Your Hearing* (Washington, DC: United States Catholic Conference, 1982). This excellent document, written by the Bishops' Committee on Priestly Life and Ministry, gives an overview of a theology of preaching, as well as some practical suggestions for preparing homilies.

[6] NCCB, *Fulfilled in Your Hearing* 7.

[7] *Gaudium et Spes* (Pastoral Constitution on the Church in the Modern World). *Vatican*

The agenda of these words from *Gaudium et Spes* could easily include the prophetic message. Karl Rahner rightfully claimed that the crisis in preaching required a theology of the annunciation of the Word of God. Preachers must become impregnated with the Word and bring it forth into the world, which is so often unwilling and sometimes hostile about receiving this message. The preacher's *fiat* in cooperating to bring the Word into the world must inspire the assembled community to speak its *fiat*. These *fiats* cannot be spoken in isolation from the concerns of the world. This mission is truly a prophetic task.

B. Confronting Individualism

An essential aspect of the prophetic task in American society is to confront the individualism that plagues our culture. Many of the ills that are at the core of our economic, social, and even ecclesial ills stem from a narcissistic individualism. The excellent book *Habits of the Heart* addresses the very issues of individualism and commitment in American life. The authors refer to Alexis de Tocqueville's thoughts in his book, *Democracy in America*:

> Alexis de Tocqueville singled out family life, our religious traditions, and our participation in local politics as helping to create the kind of person who could sustain a connection to a wider political community and thus ultimately support the maintenance of free institutions. He also warned that some aspects of our character — what he was one of the first to call "individualism" — might eventually isolate Americans from one another and thereby undermine the conditions of freedom.[8]

Council II: The Conciliar and Post Conciliar Documents, ed. Austin Flannery (Grand Rapids, MI: Eerdmans Publishing, 1992) 903.

[8] Robert N. Bellah, Richard Madsen, William Sullivan, Ann Swindler, and Steven Tipton, *Habits of the Heart* (New York: Harper and Row, 1985) vii.

When faced with this issue in society and in the Church, preachers have to decide how they will address the culture. H. Richard Niebuhr, in his book *Christ and Culture*, proposes that we have five possible alternatives.[9]

The first is to have nothing to do with the culture. This strategy calls for a total loyalty to Christ without any concern for any culture since they are all transitory. The second response is to try to bring about a marriage between religion and culture, hoping that one will enhance the other. The third is to situate religion within the culture but clearly subordinating society to religion. The fourth method is to underscore the tension that should exist between religion and culture. The final option is to view religion as an instrument for transforming the culture.

Niebuhr's second category describes most of our immigrant parents and grandparents. They came to America to be a part of the culture. Many of their religious traditions have been accepted and absorbed into American culture. Conversely, in a relatively short period of time, the culture infiltrated the churches. This becomes problematic as our society shifts more heavily to secular and materialistic values.[10]

In most instances, prophetic preaching is attempting to transform the culture. It is this goal that seems most clearly in agreement with the Gospels, the documents of the Second Vatican Council and the sentiments of the American bishops. With a renewed emphasis on the humanity of Christ, living in this world with an eye to transforming it through the values of the Gospel becomes a viable option for today's preacher. In addition, the message of the Hebrew and Christian Scriptures is a powerful one that can strongly contribute to the transformation of American society, especially with its penchant for individualism.

---

[9] H. Richard Niebuhr, *Christ and Culture* (New York: Harper Torchbooks, 1951).
[10] Anthony J. Ciorra, *Everyday Mysticism* (New York: Crossroad, 1995) 117-118.

C. Preaching: A Call to Action

A word of caution: Preachers should be careful not to use the pulpit merely to express their personal opinions. The message must clearly stem from the Scriptures and the tradition of the Church. This message must also be delivered with love for the community. St. Paul is a good model for this kind of preaching. At times he said hard things to the communities, but it was always in the context of a relationship he shared with them. Even if they disagree, people are usually willing to listen to those whom they love. Martin Luther King, Jr., said it well, "Those whom you wish to change you must first love, and they must know that you love them."

Preach without being preachy. The pulpit is not the place to give a lecture or to harangue the people. It is important that the message connect with the Scriptures that are read. It is not necessary to go into every detail of an issue. When a political stance is being taken, (e.g., about a particular war or invasion, abortion, racism and discrimination in the community, clerical financial or sexual scandals), this must be done only with much prayer, study, discernment, and consultation. When such issues are addressed, people should be given the opportunity to respond. This should not be done during the liturgy. Possibly a gathering after the liturgy or a speak-out forum could be provided on a weekday evening following the homily.

Preaching the Gospel with integrity demands that preachers overcome the fear of taking risks. There could easily be misunderstanding, rejection, and anger at the challenge of the message. It would be sad if we allowed such considerations to stifle us.

We should not forget the lessons of the many global and civil wars that have characterized the history of this past century. In almost every case too few people spoke out before it was too late. Often the Church itself so identified with the various governments involved that it did not speak out or do anything that might be considered disloyal or unpatriotic. Hopefully the Church — of which each of us is a member — has come a long way since then. Preachers must continue that momentum, especially when the government is supportive of issues such as abortion, that are contrary to the teachings of the Gospel.

Finally, and most importantly, prophetic preaching is a call to action. The preacher should be clear as to what possible actions might be taken in response to the homily. They should be sensitive to have an approach that is invitational and not condemnatory or intimidating. Prophetic preachers should propose concrete forms of action so that God's reign of peace, love, and justice might be more visible in our world.

D. Pastoral Suggestions

1. As a staff, go to a workshop or a class on preaching.
2. Read and discuss *The Prophetic Imagination* by Walter Brueggemann.
3. Conduct a "prophetic preaching" series in the parish. Prepare the people for this in advance. Topics should be announced ahead of time. Supporting articles might be printed in the bulletin. The homilies would be on the given topic and parishioners would be invited to stay after the liturgy for discussion.
4. Watch the television series, "Great Preachers," on the *Odyssey* Network.

II. EVANGELIZATION

What was from the beginning, what we have heard, what we have seen with our eyes, what we have looked upon and touched with our hands, concerning the word of life — the life was visible and we saw it, and we testify and proclaim to you the everlasting life which was with the Father and was made visible to us — what we have seen and heard we also proclaim to you so you too may be in fellowship with us (1 Jn 1:1-3).

A. The Purpose of Evangelization

The purpose of evangelization is to invite people to life. Pope John Paul II talks about a *new* evangelization, an invitation to cultures that once had a strong Catholic and religious identity to regain what they have lost. Preaching and evangelization are interconnected. Good preaching is evangelization at its best and should inspire people to become evangelizers, i.e., to take the message into the marketplace.

Jesus' preaching of the Kingdom began with a basic call to conversion, to a change of heart. "The time is fulfilled, and the Kingdom of God is at hand; repent and believe in the Gospel" (Mk 1:15) The Greek "*metanoien*" means to change one's mind, to do an about face, to come back home to God. The fundamental evil is to refuse to repent.

The early Christian communities continued in this vein. The kerygma or good news was preached. People responded with a change of heart and became a community formed by God's Word. In the second and third centuries this process became formalized in the catechumenate, which prepared people for baptism and entry into the Church. With the conversion of Constantine and the Christianization of the empire, people were baptized *en masse*. In that environment evangelization no longer centered on the kerygma, but rather was now solely identified with the conversion and baptism of pagan peoples. This approach took a variety of forms throughout the Middle Ages and basically prevailed until the time of the Second Vatican Council.

B. The Second Vatican Council and Evangelization

Prior to the Council, European theologians began to reflect on the contemporary situation. They saw formerly Christian countries becoming de-Christianized with the growth of industrialization, urbanization, and the rise of secularism and atheism. The birth of Catholic Action, the Priest Worker movement, and ecumenism gave impetus to re-situate the notion of mission within ecclesiology. New research showed that the Church as mystery and communion was primarily and essentially missionary. Vatican II gave an official stamp to these conclusions.

Lumen Gentium asserted that Christ is the light of the nations and declared that the Church's mission is to bring this light forth into the world.[11] This is to be done especially by preaching the good news to the poor, healing the contrite of heart, and saving what was lost.[12] This mission is entrusted to all the faithful:

> So, too, the laity go forth as powerful heralds of a faith in things to be hoped for (cf. Heb 1:1) provided they steadfastly join to their profession of faith a life springing from faith. This evangelization, that is, this announcing of Christ by a living testimony as well as by the spoken word, takes on a specific quality and special force in that it is carried out in the ordinary surroundings of the world.[13]

The Council saw the Church as the "universal sacrament of salvation." Its members are to share in its mission "by giving a witness to the truth, sharing with others the mystery of the heavenly Father's love."[14]

The Council's *Decree on the Missionary Activity of the Church* clearly states that "The pilgrim Church is missionary by her very nature."[15] In Chapter II on "Mission Work Itself," the *Decree* emphasizes the value of Christian witness in proclaiming the Gospel:

> For, wherever they live, all Christians are bound to show forth, by the example of their lives and by the witness

---

[11] *Lumen Gentium* 1.

[12] *Lumen Gentium* 8.

[13] *Lumen Gentium* 35.

[14] *Gaudium et Spes* 93.

[15] *Ad Gentes* (Decree on the Church's Missionary Activity). *Vatican Council II: The Conciliar and Post Conciliar Documents*, ed. Austin Flannery (Grand Rapids, MI: Eerdmans Publishing, 1992) 2.

of their speech, that new man which they put on at baptism, and that power of the Holy Spirit by whom they were strengthened at confirmation. Thus other men, observing their good works, can glorify the Father and can better perceive the real meaning of human life and the bond which ties the whole community of mankind together.[16]

The document goes on to specify some of these good works, such as the "proper regulation of the affairs of economic and social life... the education of children... waging war on famine, ignorance and disease."[17]

The Council, then, summarized and developed much of the thinking about the Church's mission that had been evolving over several decades. There was, however, no systematic theological synthesis of the Church's mission of evangelization.

The decade following the Council was a time of rapid change and transformation both for society and the Church. New nations in Africa and older ones in Latin America were seeking independence and liberation from exploitation and colonial rule. The Council's reforms of the Church's institutional structures and liturgical life were being implemented and people were searching for a deeper, more focused interior life. It also was clear by this point that we were living in the post-Christian era. Society and culture were no longer functioning with foundational Christian values and goals.

The Church now stood on the very threshold of a great spiritual-moral renewal based on the gradual rediscovery of the evangelical spirit and life which she herself shares in communion with the glorified Lord Jesus. With the publication of *Evangelii nuntiandi* on December 8, 1974, Pope Paul VI endeavored to give a new impetus to this evangelical renewal and mission.

---

[16] *Ad Gentes* 11.
[17] *Ad Gentes* 12.

C. Evangelization and the Parish Community

As a result of the Vatican Council and the writings of Pope Paul VI and Pope John Paul II, there has been a renewed appreciation of the importance of evangelization. Many parishes are currently attempting to address this issue and are seeking ways to incorporate the principles of evangelization in their local communities. We begin by stating some of the key principles and theological underpinnings of evangelization.

First, the essential truth of evangelization is that human beings are invited to be in a relationship with God. Religious experience is at the core of this message. An important nuance is that love precedes knowledge. Bernard Lonergan wrote, "Before it enters the world mediated by meaning, religion is the prior word God speaks to us by flooding our hearts with his love."[18] This approach is modeled on the experience of the preaching of the early Church where people witnessed to their experience of God and invited others to share in that experience by becoming a part of their fellowship.

Second, important to this process of evangelization is not only the teaching of the truth (orthodoxy) but also an invitation to a way of living in conformity with that truth (orthopraxis). Thus, a moral-spiritual life must follow from the initial experience of God's love. The early Christian community invited others to a way of life that was characterized by fellowship or *koinonia*. They were essentially a Eucharistic community. Once a person was baptized into this community a change of behavior was called for. This change was fueled by the vision of the beatitudes, which gave Christians a definite way of living life in the world. The community and its life around the Eucharistic table reinforced this vision of a life lived out of love.

Third, evangelization happens in two moments. God com-

---

[18] For an excellent study of the relationship between religious experience and the study of theology, see Bernard Lonergan, *Method in Theology* (Toronto: University of Toronto Press, 1971) 101-125.

municates love, and we respond by accepting that love and embracing a particular lifestyle. This viewpoint impacts the way we do theology. Scholastic theology separated systematic theology from spiritual and moral theology. Evangelization demands that these various disciplines be integrated. In other words, evangelizing others into the community does not begin with intellectual or academic truths. It begins with an experience of God through the lifestyle of the faith community and its individual members. As people are attracted by the vibrancy of the love manifested in the community of believers, they are then invited to learn about the beliefs and spiritual-moral lifestyle of the disciples of Jesus Christ.

Given this background, the first call to pastoral ministers is to be evangelized themselves. They need to be renewed in their relationship with the Lord. They also need to confront their lifestyle with basic scriptural principles such as those expressed in the beatitudes as a measuring rod. From this experience and the testimony of their lives, they can then go forth to invite others to communion with the Lord through their relationship with the community.

As the parish staff and others in the community are evangelized, they need to strategize on how to approach the evangelization process in the parish. Wherever possible, it is good to think of evangelization in terms of families. This is the basic social unit. It would be an excellent contribution to families to invite them as a group to join together in the faith journey. This can be done while respecting differences in ages and spiritual development. Parish ministers need to assure families that it is all right to be in different places on the journey and still come together to support one another.

Here are just a few examples of how this might be accomplished. We can begin by encouraging families to pray together. We can do this by providing them with meal prayers and other prayer formats that they can share together. We can teach families how to read the Bible together. This can be a very simple process. They can read a brief Bible story, share a thought or a reaction, and close with a prayer. Parishes should provide family liturgies for the Sunday Eucharist. If possible, it is an excellent idea occasionally to have people break into groups according to age for the Liturgy of the Word and then come together as families to share what happened. This can be a beautiful and profitable way of celebrating the Liturgy of the Word before gathering together for the Liturgy of the Eucharist. This is a concrete experience in the parish where the dynamic and value of family can be reinforced.

Finally, Paul VI and John Paul II in their emphasis on a new evangelization have made it clear that all Christians have an urgent role in evangelizing our culture. In our parishes, we need to identify those who are ready to evangelize, as well as those who need to be evangelized. In that setting, the focus on family is a great place to start. It is not the only place, but certainly one that is worthwhile pursuing. If families strong in the faith are formed in our parishes, the parish community will come alive and will have many cell units where the Church's moral teaching is received, supported, and lived.

D. Pastoral Suggestions

1. Have special liturgies where the focus is on the family. Choose special occasions or feasts that lend themselves to family gatherings.
2. Parish staff and select parishioners should be offered the opportunity for training in evangelization.
3. Become acquainted with local television, radio, and newspaper personnel. Publicize your parish events.
4. Have a "Disenchanted Evening" where fallen away Catholics can come to the parish to discuss their hurts and questions. The little volume by Lorene Hanley Duquin, *Could You Ever Come Back to the Catholic Church?* (NY: Alba House, 1997) provides an excellent non-threatening way to reach out to them and provides a lot of answers to the questions and hurts they may have.

5. Discuss the various papal documents and those of the American bishops on evangelization.

III. YOUNG ADULTS

It is almost impossible to speak about family and not include the problems of our young people. More and more parishes are starting to include their concerns high on their list of priorities. It is obvious that members of the younger generations are often absent from our faith assemblies. One of the reasons they do not come to church is that they often find the parish structure too large and impersonal. Many of the Pentecostal or evangelical churches provide them with a challenge, an opportunity to become involved, and the warmth and intimacy that they long for. In response to this we would propose that the small faith group structure responds best to these needs for intimacy, acceptance and involvement which young people often find lacking in the larger parish community.

Coupled with this, many young people are unaware of the Church's moral teachings or think they are unrealistic or too "out of touch." Because the voice of our culture speaks so loudly to them, many are amoral. It is a bleak picture. However, as the International Youth Rallies with the Holy Father have proved, these same young people are looking to be challenged. They are highly idealistic in many of their aspirations and are just waiting for someone not to condemn them but to reach out to them with love.

A. A Proposal from the American Bishops

With this in mind, the American bishops in their pastoral plan for young adults recognized the crisis we face. Many young adults feel alienated from the Church, while others are oblivious to the Church's teachings. The bishops begin by saying, "We acknowledge the pain many of you speak of in feeling unwelcome and alone — strangers in the house of God. For this lack of hospitality we apologize and promise anew greater efforts to welcome you into Church life." They also quote Pope John Paul II's message to young adults at a World Youth Day Mass in 1995: "Open the Gospel and discover that Jesus Christ wants to be your friend. He wants to be your companion at every stage on the road of life."

The Holy Father and the bishops have set a definite tone in how we must begin in reaching out to young people. We need to understand that many of them are unaware of the teachings of the faith and are misinformed regarding its moral teachings. We must be compassionate and understanding, recognizing that in many instances this is due to no fault of their own. Our secular culture, the absence of strong family ties, and insufficient teaching are some of the factors that contribute to this malaise.

In their pastoral the bishops note the following trends:

1. With the birth of their first child, young adults typically return to the active religious practice after a decline in Church participation during late adolescence and their early twenties. Today, this return is no longer certain. If they do return, it can be with great tentativeness.

2. Many Catholic men and women tell of not feeling welcomed into our communities while others speak of wanting, but not finding, the Church's help with serious moral and economic questions.

3. The membership of many, if not most, of our Catholic organizations is much older today than it was 20 years ago.

4. Inter-church marriages, both ecumenical and inter-religious, have increased. This ultimately affects Church life, especially as a couple decides which faith community to join and in which tradition to raise their children.

5. The values of many young adults no longer come primarily from family and Church, but from friends, the media and contemporary society.

Given these realities, the bishops strongly urge that we be especially sensitive to welcome young people into the community.

It is our responsibility to create an atmosphere in which their faith is "nurtured and strengthened." In making this happen ministers should be open and flexible.

An important point they make is that "while some alienation stems from disagreement over Church teachings, much of what young adults feel regarding the institutional Church arises from a misunderstanding of what the Church actually teaches. Many young adults told us that what is most convincing is an open but well-reasoned discussion, informed and fortified by the minister's confidence in the wisdom of the Church."[19]

B. Begin by Listening

Given what the bishops have written, we have an approach that we can use in transmitting the moral values of the Church to the younger generations. First, we have to go out and meet them. We need to invite them into the Church. We need to find them where they are, whether this is on the Internet, in the shopping malls, or at the workplace.

The starting point needs to be listening. We need to listen to their life experience, their questions and their needs. We must do this in a non-judgmental way. Their life experience and behavior might be jolting to us due to the cultural and generational gap between us. Things that we hold sacred such as belief in Jesus Christ, the Eucharist, the moral and social teachings of the Church, etc. may have very little, if any, meaning to younger generations. The conversation must begin with our understanding and accepting them where they are. Above all, they must know that we care about them and will continue to love them no matter what. They are part

---

[19] U.S. Bishops, *Renewing the Vision* (Washington, DC: United States Catholic Conference, 1997). The entire text is worth reading and studying by parish staffs. It gives an excellent summary of the attitudes of today's youth and a Catholic vision of ministry for them.

of our community regardless of what their opinions or actions might be.

The bishops set the tone in approaching them in this way. Interestingly enough, they say this even with respect to marriage preparation. They point out that young adults approach the Church to be married for a number of reasons. "Regardless of why they come, the Church and its ministers need to welcome them as Christ welcomes them, with understanding, love, and acceptance, challenging them with the Gospel message, and giving them hope that a lifelong commitment is possible." Please note the pastoral tone of this statement. In the past, some clergy gave young people a hard time if they lived an ambivalent faith life. The current document recognizes that you "catch more flies with honey" and that it is important to "get a foot into the door."

C. An Invitation to Conversion

At the same time, Church ministers should invite young people to a relationship with Jesus Christ. This is the beginning of the moral life. In Dostoyevsky's novel, *The Brothers Karamazov*, Ivan expresses the attitude that if God does not exist, then everything is permissible. Belief in God and a relationship with Jesus Christ is the foundation of the moral life. These beliefs give us a reason to be moral, and young people need a reason. Morality is not voted upon or dependent upon our needs for self-fulfillment. God is the author of the moral life, and it is God who makes moral demands upon us.

Pope John Paul II takes this approach in his encyclical *Veritatis Splendor*. He begins with a beautiful reflection on Matthew 19:16, "Teacher, what must I do?" Being a disciple of Christ is the foundation of Christian morality. Jesus is the one who fully reveals the mystery of God and how we should live life. He is the ultimate norm against which we need to measure our decisions and behaviors.

What we are inviting young people to is to conversion. The fact that we are speaking to them testifies that the Spirit is already at work. Their willingness to enter into conversation with us is a sign of the Spirit's presence. The underlying theological assumption is that God is the One who initiates the process of conversion. It is from this belief that we can have the courage to present Jesus to them with conviction. Young people need role models. We can draw from people in our tradition who have struggled and later accepted God's invitation to a life of faith. The saints — and there are many with whom they can relate, who were both young and modern in their outlook — can be very attractive figures for the young who are struggling with life and faith issues. Most important, however, is that *we* witness to them by *our* lives. In calling young people to conversion, it is not intellectual facts or arguments that will draw them but rather autobiographical accounts of real people who accepted Jesus as their Lord and Savior and the difference that this made in their lives.

The following of Jesus is demanding. This should never be watered down. The challenge of the beatitudes, which are the heart of the Christian life, should be the starting point from which we begin to teach about living the Gospel life. Once this is established, the moral teachings of the Church should be clearly presented. Certainly, sexual ethics are an essential part of this presentation. We must be careful, however, not to limit morality to this. All life issues, as well as the social and economic teachings of the Church must be included in the conversation, beginning — as the *Catechism* does — with the ten commandments.

Having taught these with clarity, we need to recognize that not all will be ready to accept these teachings. Even though there might not be a meeting of the minds, there should be an acceptance of the person. The underlying principle is that conversion is oftentimes gradual and is always ongoing. The door should always be left open. Although the principles of conscience formation and disagreement should be discussed, these should not be the center point of our teaching to the young. We should aim to create a balance between clear communication of the truth while respecting the individual who might make choices or decisions that do not as yet reflect an appropriation of those truths.

Finally, let us look at the question of forgiveness. Young people need to know that all is forgivable, that God's love is prodigal. Past mistakes, as well as future mistakes, can be reconciled. No matter what happens, a forgiving God and a loving community will always be there for them. It is this welcoming and loving God that parish ministers must invite young people to get to know and love.

D. Pastoral Suggestions

1. Discuss the possibility of hiring a youth minister. Be clear on job description and goals. If your parish cannot afford this, think of the possibilities of a youth ministry team.
2. Plan large gatherings for youth on the deanery and even diocesan levels.
3. Have pilgrimage opportunities for youth to religious shrines or places where religious artists or musicians are performing.
4. Plan retreats and other community experiences for the youth of the parish. This might be done with clusters of parishes.
5. Provide opportunities for youth to volunteer their services on a regular basis. Vacation time offers the possibility of extended volunteer experiences at home as well as in other parts of the country.

IV. THE SMALL GROUP PROCESS

A. The Phenomena of the Small Group Experience

The small group is one of the ways that American parishes are attempting to nurture a family atmosphere. The large communities of the past are frequently no longer meeting the needs of many of our people. As we have said "community" is the symbol that the post-Vatican II Church is attempting to emphasize in its ecclesiology, liturgy, and social teachings. As a result, the small group experience is a growing phenomenon in the contemporary Catholic experience. To name just a few, Renew, Small Faith Communities, RCIA, and Parish Based Bible Studies are places where the small group experience is growing quickly in our parishes.

It is important to recognize that the small group process is not just a passing fad, but the recovery of an essential ecclesial element. Christianity actually began with the small group experience. Christians gathered in homes where they reflected on God's Word and broke bread together. The Acts of the Apostles is filled with examples of this kind of interaction. The first impulse of what we now call religious life came when Christianity was accepted as the religion of the empire in the fourth century. The earliest monastic movements of the fourth and fifth centuries were urges to recapture the earlier, more intimate and focused experience of the early Christian communities.[20]

This impulse continued well into the Middle Ages. Lay communities called Beguines and Beghards were associations of lay people without formal vows who gathered in small groups for prayer, community, and ministry. The religious guilds of the Middle Ages are a further example of people who gathered in small communities for prayer and to support one another in doing works of charity.

Many of the religious orders began in this way. In some instances they grew to such large numbers that the Church imposed a rule and structure of life upon them in order to ensure that particular charisms would be preserved in the Church.

---

[20] Max Delesspesse, *The Church Community, Leaven and Lifestyle* (Ottawa: The Catholic Center of St. Paul University, 1968) 16.

B. Small Groups in Today's Church

The dynamic and interaction that occurs among participants in small groups is still something that many people and movements find attractive and helpful. In recent years over 100,000 small Christian communities have emerged throughout the world.[21] In the United States alone, over 15 million adults gather in small groups for religious purposes.[22]

Among the reasons for this phenomenal growth is the fact that much in our culture is not supportive of Christian values. The pressures of consumerism and materialism are so strong that it is almost impossible not to get caught up in them. Small groups provide support to live according to the values of the Gospel. The industrialization of our society has shaken people in many ways. The Secretariat for Promoting Christian Unity reports that "a breakdown of traditional social structures, cultural patterns, and traditional sets of values, caused by industrialization, urbanization, migration, rapid development of communication systems, all-rational technocratic systems, etc., leave many individuals confused, uprooted, insecure, and therefore vulnerable."[23] The dramatic shifts and uncertainties in our economy also force people to once again ask the basic questions about our priorities and the meaning and purpose of life.

All of these factors contribute to the contemporary search for meaning and spirituality in the midst of tremendous uncertainty. And it is within the structure of the small group that this most often happens. Regardless of whether the small group is RCIA, Bible Study, or Parish Based Support Groups, we need to look at the common denominators. In addition, we need to use these opportunities to present the values and moral teachings of the Church.

---

[21] Vatican Secretariat for Promoting Christian Unity, *Sects or New Religious Movements in the World: Pastoral Challenges*, USCC, May 3, 1986, pp. 12-13.

[22] *Ibid.*

[23] *Op. cit.*, p. 13.

C. *What Happens in Small Groups?*

The small group is a place where people feel accepted and not threatened. They can begin to let their guard down and express what is really on their minds. It is important that people feel free to voice their questions, confusion, and concerns. Part of the function of the small group is to be supportive of people in their needs. What happens in this initial phase is that relationships begin to form.

Rather than beginning with the truths and doctrines of the Church, it is better to allow people to share their experiences. Models of theological reflection can help people look at their experiences in the light of contemporary culture.[24] Most often, the reality beneath peoples' experiences is a searching for God. Oftentimes they do not even realize this. At some point in the process this should be made explicit.

Within Christian groups, it is important that the word of God be introduced. Participants should be invited to share what the word means to them. The objective meaning of the word should also be presented. This is an excellent moment to introduce the fact that the word challenges us to certain actions and behaviors.

It is important to remember that people do not have to learn everything at once. Oftentimes, there will be resistance to the teachings of the Church. Faithfulness to the relationships within the group and consistently calling people back to the Lord and the Gospels allows the gradual process of conversion and learning to unfold.

---

[24] The following are some suggestions for further study and explanation of theological reflection for the parish setting: Patricia O'Connell Killen and John DeBeer, *The Art of Theological Reflection* (New York: Crossroad, 1994); Monika Hellwig, *Whose Experience Counts in Theological Reflection* (Milwaukee: Marquette University Press, 1987); James D. Whitehead and Evelyn Eaton Whitehead, *Method in Ministry* (New York: Harper and Row, 1985); Robert L. Kinast, "Moving Theological Reflection from Field Education to the Parish," *Chicago Studies* 31 (April 1992): 93-106. Also, The Center for Theological Reflection has helpful materials upon request: P.O. Box 86035, Madeira Beach, Florida 33738-6035; telephone 813-397-5477.

The method presented here is based on the principles of adult learning and faith development.

> Adults learn best when treated with respect and when the learning draws upon the wealth of their past experience. Adults learn best when they are physically comfortable and in social learning groups (either one-to-one or small groups of peers). Adults learn best when there are opportunities for a variety of activities, in a problem-centered situation, when a question needs resolution, when a task needs doing, when they see progress and immediate results for the time they are putting into learning.[25]

These are ideal settings in which to introduce issues of sexual mores, medical ethics, and the social teachings of recent papal encyclicals. People are disposed to learning in this environment. They have the freedom here to express their questions, reservations, and personal experiences. They have been primed to enter more deeply into the Christian mysteries. Catechists, RCIA leaders, and group leaders have a wonderful opportunity for calling people to deeper conversion through examining their behavior in the light of the Gospel in the context of a supportive and loving faith community.

Small group opportunities in our parishes can support our preaching and evangelizing. These groups give people a way of "going to the next step" and to formulate plans of action. The power of the small group experience is that the process can go on for a lifetime. It can become a permanent structure within the parish that can support and enliven every aspect of the parish's mission and goals.

---

[25] DeBoy 75-78

D. Pastoral Suggestions

1. The parish staff should be trained in the basic principles of group dynamics.
2. Explore the possibilities for *Renew*, family-centered catechesis, or other small group vehicles for evangelization or religious instruction.
3. Offer Bible study opportunities. Consider doing this after one of the Sunday liturgies when larger numbers of people are present.
4. Using *Shorter Christian Prayer*, have public Morning and Evening Prayer in the parish church as often as possible.[26]

V. RECONCILIATION

A. The Catholic Tradition of Forgiveness

We all fall short of the mark. We need to reaffirm the Catholic tradition that is not one of condemnation but rather ongoing reconciliation. We end this chapter with reconciliation because it must always be included as an essential element of Catholic moral teaching. Catholic teaching upholds the highest moral standards and at the same time acknowledges our human weakness and need for mercy.

This spirit is captured in the words of absolution in the new Rite of Reconciliation. They contain a powerful message of hope for the world:

> God, the Father of mercies through the death and resurrection of his Son has reconciled the world to himself and sent the Holy Spirit among us for the forgiveness of sins; through the ministry of the Church may

---

[26] *Shorter Christian Prayer* (NY: Catholic Book Publishing Co., 1988).

God give you pardon and peace, and I absolve you from
your sins in the name of the Father, and of the Son, and
of the Holy Spirit.[27]

The theology of the paschal mystery is paramount in these
beautiful words. The emphasis is on what God is doing. It is the
God who is the Father of mercies, the God who is always ready to
forgive and who initiates the process of forgiveness. It is important to remember when people stray from the moral teachings of
the Church that it is God who conspires to bring them back. We
may abandon God but God never abandons us.

B. God's Unconditional Love

The poem and story that follow place reconciliation within
the context of God's unconditional love. We choose to do what is
right because God loves us so much. When we fail, we go back to
the God who is always ready to welcome us home. The poem was
written in England and refers to the city of Birmingham. Think
of this as any one of our large American cities.

> When Jesus came to Golgotha,
> They hanged him on a tree.
> They drove great nails
> through hands and feet,
> And made a Calvary.
>
> They crowned him with a crown of thorns,
> Red were his wounds and deep;
> For those were crude and cruel days,
> And human flesh was cheap.
>
> When Jesus came to Birmingham
> They simply passed him by.

---

[27] *The Rites of the Catholic Church*, vol. 1 (New York: Pueblo Publishing Co., 1976)
546-547.

They never hurt a hair of him,
They only let him die.

For men had grown more tender,
And they would not give him pain;
They only passed down the street
And left him in the rain.

Still Jesus cried, "Forgive them,
For they know not what they do."
And still it rained a winter rain
That drenched him through and through.

The crowds went home and left the streets,
Without a soul to see.
And Jesus crouched against the wall
And cried for Calvary.[28]

The story is also about the power of tears. Walter Wagerin shares this touching experience about his little son Matthew. When Matthew decided to do something, he just dashed headlong in and did what he wanted to do without too much thinking of the consequences. So one day, Walter relates, he went into his son's room and found him sitting on the bed with a whole stack of comic books around him. He said to Matthew, "Where did you get the comic books?" Matthew said, "I took them out of the library." "You took them out of the library?" "Yes." "You mean you stole them from the library?" "Yes." So the father called the librarian and said that he was going to march his son Matthew right down with the comic books to apologize and restore what he had stolen. He did precisely that and the librarian gave little Matthew a stern lecture about stealing.

The following summer they vacationed at a small community in Vermont where there was a general store. When they returned home after the summer, at the beginning of the fall, the father went into Matthew's room and found a pile of comic books

---

[28] Quoted by William J. Bausch, *More Telling Stories* (Mystic, CT: Twenty-Third Publications, 1994) 22.

in his dresser drawer. And Matthew said, "I stole them from the store this summer." So the father took the comic books and he went into the den and started a fire in the fireplace and he threw the comic books into the flames, and with each comic book that he threw into the flames, he reminded little Matthew of the seventh commandment, "Thou shalt not steal."

A year later, Matthew again stole some comic books, and this time his father told him that he was going to have to spank him. He brought him into the study and put him over his knee, and spanked him five times with his bare hand. Why five times? Because he felt that if he did any less he would be too soft and if he was really angry he might do too many, so he limited himself to five. He spanked Matthew and he sat him down, and he could see his son's head hanging; it was obvious that Matthew did not want to shed a tear in front of his father. The father understood that. And so not wanting to see little Matthew cry he said, "Matthew, I'm going to leave you alone for a while, but I'll be back in a few minutes." After he had stepped out of the room and closed the door behind him, the father himself began to cry. Then he went into the bathroom and washed his face and went back into his study and talked to his little son Matthew.

Years later when Matthew was a teenager and he and his mother were driving back from a shopping trip, as often happened, they were reminiscing. And the reminiscence happened to come around to those early days when Matthew was a rascal stealing comic books. Matthew said to his mother, "You know, after that incident with Dad, I really never stole anything again." And his mother commented, "I suppose the reason was because your father spanked you." "Oh, no," Matthew replied, "It was because when he stepped out of the room I could hear him crying."[29]

There is a power in knowing that we are loved. The last thing anyone of us would want to do would be to hurt someone whom we loved. We are not proposing that an unhealthy guilt should be

---

[29] Bausch 24-25.

the motivating factor in calling someone to repentance. There is a sorrow in God's heart when we stray from his love and make choices contrary to what is good. The root of that sorrow is that we are not living up to our potential; we are not fulfilling the purposes for which God created us. God has a passion for us. That passion is frustrated when we sin. A healthy sense of guilt would lead us back into the arms of the God who weeps for us and is waiting with open arms. But we must respond by admitting our sinfulness, by naming what we have done. This becomes our act of worship of the Father.

The words of absolution speak of the "death and resurrection of his Son." Christ is the one who shows us how to be faithful to the Father. He is totally obedient to all that the Father asks. In our presentation of Christ, it is important not to underestimate the struggle that Jesus endured all along the way. This approach is advantageous in presenting the challenges of the moral life, especially to young people. They need to know that it is acceptable to struggle and that God is in the struggle. They also need to know that God's grace through the power of the "death and resurrection of the Lord Jesus" is with them.

The absolution continues, "He reconciled the world to himself and sent the Holy Spirit among us for the forgiveness of sins." This acknowledges the fact that God's love is greater than our sinfulness. There is nothing we can do to destroy that reality. Ultimately, goodness and truth will prevail. In the sacrament we are merely claiming and accepting in our own lives what Christ has already accomplished. This is the power that we offer to people through the grace of reconciliation.

C. Walking Together Again with God and One Another

Reconciliation means to "walk together again." No matter what we have done, if we acknowledge our sin, we can walk together with God. This happens "through the ministry of the Church." So, we now walk together with the entire community of believers once again. God grants us "pardon and peace." It is only here that we receive that "peace which the world cannot give, that peace which is beyond all understanding." The tangible sign of what has occurred is expressed through the laying on of hands and the epiclesis, "I absolve you from your sins, in the name of the Father, and of the Son, and of the Holy Spirit." This is a moment of tremendous happiness for "there is more joy in heaven over one sinner who repents than over ninety-nine just persons."

A renaissance for the sacrament of reconciliation is sorely needed in our parishes. It is no secret that this dimension of Catholic life is being used less and less by our people. It is the task of parish ministers to provide welcoming atmospheres and meaningful, well-prepared experiences of this sacrament in our faith communities. As the moral life is taken more and more seriously, a healthy, positive use of the sacrament of reconciliation will be increasingly important.

At the same time, we need to be clear that individual reconciliation is not the only way that God's forgiveness is experienced. Sacramentally, the Church allows for other expressions of the rite through communal penance services and general absolution.[30] The Eucharistic liturgy begins with reconciliation. Two Eucharistic Prayers are entirely about this theme.

Even more basic is the reconciliation that should take place within the relationships of our parishes. Whether it is parish staffs, families, parish councils and other groups within a parish, we are all in need of reconciliation. Sacramental reconciliation will not be meaningful in today's society unless we live reconciliation in our relationships.

[30] *The Rites of the Catholic Church*, vol. 1, 519-544. The instructions, norms, and regulations for the use of the various forms for the Rite of Penance are given here.

D. Pastoral Suggestions

1. Reflect on how often individual reconciliation is offered in your parish and how the sacrament is celebrated.
2. Offer quality experiences of communal reconciliation during Advent and Lent.
3. Reflect on the connection between reconciliation and the Eucharist. Offer expanded and more elaborate penitential rites at special times during the liturgical year.[31]
4. Consider making more public invitations from the pulpit, inviting parishioners to celebrate the sacrament of reconciliation.

VI. CONCLUSION

Finally, the preaching of the goals of the moral life calls for a prophet who is not afraid to challenge. The final word, however, is not a hard word, it is a gentle word: "Come to me all you who are weary and find life burdensome, and I will refresh you. Take my yoke upon your shoulders and learn from me, for I am gentle and humble of heart. Your souls will find rest, for my yoke is easy and my burden light" (Mt 11:28-30). Preaching, teaching, and evangelizing are about humility and gentleness. We need to be humble always to remember that it is God's Kingdom, not ours. If we believe that, we can go about the task of renewing the moral life with a gentle urgency. Urgent because our parishes so badly need this right now. Gentle because it is a God of compassion, patience, and reconciliation who is calling people, both young and old, to a relationship with himself and a way of life in the world that mirrors his goodness.

---

[31] Peter E. Fink, *Praying the Sacraments* (Washington, DC: The Pastoral Press, 1991). Fink has an excellent chapter, "Investigating the Sacrament of Penance," that clearly defines the relationship between Eucharist and Penance.